This Book Belongs to...

____

...a Woman Seeking God's Wisdom

Proverbs *for a* Woman's Day

Elizabeth George

HARVEST HOUSE PUBLISHERS
EUGENE, OREGON

Unless otherwise indicated, all Scripture quotations are from the New American Standard Bible, © 1960, 1962, 1963, 1968, 1971, 1972, 1973, 1975, 1977, 1995 by The Lockman Foundation. Used by permission. (www.Lockman.org)

Verses marked NKJV are taken from the New King James Version®. Copyright © 1982 by Thomas Nelson, Inc. Used by permission. All rights reserved.

Verses marked NIV are taken from the Holy Bible, New International Version®, NIV®. Copyright © 1973, 1978, 1984, 2011 by Biblica, Inc.® Used by permission. All rights reserved worldwide.

Verses marked RSV are taken from the Revised Standard Version of the Bible, copyright © 1946, 1952, 1971 by the Division of Christian Education of the National Council of the Churches of Christ in the U.S.A. Used by permission. All rights reserved.

Verses marked NLT are taken from the *Holy Bible*, New Living Translation, copyright © 1996, 2004, 2007, 2013, 2015 by Tyndale House Foundation. Used by permission of Tyndale House Publishers, Inc., Carol Stream, Illinois 60188. All rights reserved.

Verses marked ESV are from The ESV® Bible (The Holy Bible, English Standard Version®) copyright © 2001 by Crossway, a publishing ministry of Good News Publishers. Used by permission. All rights reserved.

Verses marked KNOX are from the KNOX BIBLE, *The Holy Bible: A Translation from the Latin Vulgate in the Light of the Hebrew and Greek Originals* by Monsignor Ronald Knox. Copyright © 1954 Westminster Diocese.

Cover by Koechel Peterson & Associates, Minneapolis, Minnesota

Cover Image © Snezh / Shutterstock

PROVERBS FOR A WOMAN'S DAY

Copyright © 2017 by Elizabeth George

Published by Harvest House Publishers
Eugene, Oregon 97402
www.harvesthousepublishers.com

ISBN 978-0-7369-5124-1 (pbk.)
ISBN 978-0-7369-5125-8 (eBook)

Library of Congress Cataloging-in-Publication Data
Names: George, Elizabeth, 1944- author.
Title: Proverbs for a woman's day : living everyday life God's way / Elizabeth George.
Description: Eugene, Oregon : Harvest House Publishers, 2017.
Identifiers: LCCN 2016044553 (print) | LCCN 2016051021 (ebook) | ISBN 9780736951241 (pbk.) | ISBN 9780736951258 (ebook)
Subjects: LCSH: Bible. Proverbs—Criticism, interpretation, etc. | Christian women—Religious life.
Classification: LCC BS1465.52 .G46 2017 (print) | LCC BS1465.52 (ebook) | DDC 248.8/43—dc23
LC record available at https://lccn.loc.gov/2016044553

All rights reserved. No part of this publication may be reproduced, stored in a retrieval system, or transmitted in any form or by any means—electronic, mechanical, digital, photocopy, recording, or any other—except for brief quotations in printed reviews, without the prior permission of the publisher.

Printed in the United States of America

17 18 19 20 21 22 23 24 25 / BP-GL / 10 9 8 7 6 5 4 3 2 1

Contents

Dear Seeker of God's Wisdom...

Do you work in the world and struggle with the way things are done or not done? Could you use some help in your relationships? Do you have children to raise but aren't sure what to do, or is what you are doing not working? How many times a day are you uncertain about the decisions you make? Well, good news! God has all the answers you are seeking in the book of Proverbs.

Welcome...and thank you for joining me in a practical and devotional journey through the book of Proverbs. My love for this book of the Bible began just days after becoming a Christian. I give thanks to God daily that my husband, Jim, and I were directed to a church filled with people who not only had Bibles, but were actually following along as the pastor in the pulpit was preaching.

After our first experience of such thrilling teaching, Jim and I went to the church's prayer room. The caring people there gave us a Bible reading schedule and advised us to start reading through the Bible...which then meant we needed Bibles!

We charged immediately from the prayer room to the church bookstore where we purchased two matching Bibles, and the next morning we cracked open our brand-new Bibles and started reading at Genesis 1:1.

Not long after we started reading every morning in our Bibles, we were instructed while attending a Bible conference to read one chapter of Proverbs daily—the chapter that corresponded to the day of the month. For instance, if the day of the month was the third, we were to read Proverbs 3. The conference leader explained that reading from the book of Proverbs daily would give direction for our *practical lives*, just as reading in the Psalms daily would give direction for our *devotional lives*.

And it's true! The book of Proverbs is God's counsel from above for your conduct and mine here below. By reading one chapter of Proverbs every day, we receive inspired words from God on the ways of the world—and how to live a godly life in the midst of it. As Proverbs 1:3 states, one result of reading Proverbs is "to receive instruction in wise behavior." Knowing how desperately I needed this kind of help, I started that very day reading one chapter of Proverbs daily.

As I faithfully continued my repeated journeys through the book of Proverbs, I learned a practical reality: Proverbs is loaded with down-to-earth sayings of truth that are meant to be lingered over—to be pondered and savored. They are meant to cause you and me to think through their advice and implications for the challenges of busy, intense, everyday life. It wasn't long before I began noting and marking topics in the margins of my Bible—topics and verses that were just for women like you and me.

After 40-plus years of reading Proverbs most every day, I am seeking in this book to share heart-to-heart with you as a woman. I am drawing from my personal markings, study notes, and applications from the 31 chapters of Proverbs. I've handpicked a selected number of topics that I have benefited from as a woman, wife, mother, and daughter. And it was pure joy to write an opening prayer for each chapter. These prayers were written from my heart and are intended to be prayed by you from your heart to our heavenly Father as you approach His wisdom each day.

Dear reading friend, I am praying that you will fall in love with the book of Proverbs! That you will embrace its instructions. That you will grow in God's wisdom and be blessed as you use and apply it in your daily living. That each day you will want to learn more from this refreshing, practical, and powerful book in the Bible.

> *Listen to me,*
> *for blessed are they who keep my ways.*
> *Heed instruction and be wise,*
> *and do not neglect it.*
> *Blessed is the man who listens to me,*
> *watching daily at my gates,*
> *waiting at my doorposts.*

For he who finds me finds life
and obtains favor from the LORD.
(Proverbs 8:32-35)

In His everlasting love,

Elizabeth George

P.S.
For more in-depth study, I have provided questions for you or for a group study on my website, ElizabethGeorge.com, and a list of books and commentaries that will help you understand more about the book of Proverbs in the back of this book. Happy reading and growth in the wisdom of Proverbs.

EG

1

Beginning Your Every Day —Wisdom—

To know wisdom and instruction,
to discern the sayings of understanding,
to receive instruction in wise behavior,
righteousness, justice and equity.
PROVERBS 1:2-3

A Prayer to Pray—

Father of all wisdom and the all-wise One, my heart gives thanks to You for caring for your creation enough to make sure we are fully equipped to handle the days of our lives. As I think about this day, O Lord, and all that is planned, all that is necessary—and all the temptations and interruptions and crises that may come my way, I ask You afresh, "Lord, give me wisdom! I need it to manage this day in a way that pleases You and bears the mark of Your wisdom on it. Amen."

I still adore the movie *The Sound of Music*—and so do my two daughters. We have great memories of watching it together and singing along with its many unforgettable tunes. Talk about a wonderful classic! Do you remember Maria teaching the von Trapp children the basics of music by asking them to "start at the very beginning"?

Learning the many wise sayings in the book of Proverbs also requires that we start at the beginning. Prepare yourself to be blessed by the beauty and practicality of God's wisdom for your every day.

A Journey Through Proverbs

When as a brand-new Christian I was advised to seriously consider reading one chapter of Proverbs every day, I simply started! I was so eager to grow as a Christian that I hadn't realized that people's suggestions might be optional! All I can say is I thank God each time I open up the book of Proverbs to receive fresh wisdom for my day. I praise Him that He moved my heart to desire to participate in this sweet, simple, life-changing ritual of spending about two minutes every day reading one chapter of God's wisdom for my life...and my day.

The day that I started reading Proverbs was the nineteenth day of the month, so I began with Proverbs, chapter 19. Wanting to be faithful, I read every day for the remainder of the month, wading through the last half of Proverbs for the very first time...and started right back over again the next day—Day 1 of the next month.

Every single day I felt like falling on my knees before God in thanksgiving for what I was learning from the book of Proverbs! At last I was finding real help and guidance for some of my ongoing problems. In addition, I was cataloging a great number of practical how-tos for daily living.

I have to admit there was lots of confusion and head-scratching over the meaning of many of the proverbs. They were like riddles to me. But in time an amazing thing happened: The more I read, the more I saw, and the more I saw, the more I understood. I began to get it, to understand it! And I found that each month when I started back through Proverbs, more new life-changing truths jumped out at me. Without even realizing it, I actually memorized several key proverbs. They just stuck in my soul and were with me every minute to guide and encourage me!

Several years later I graduated to reading through Proverbs each day with the added information provided in the notes in a study Bible. And it wasn't long before I was supplementing my daily reading of Proverbs with full volumes of commentaries on the book of Proverbs. This very minute as I am writing this chapter, my side table is strewn with at least 13 volumes devoted to verse-by-verse study of every verse in the book of Proverbs. (See bibliography on page 277.)

Looking back, my journey of studying through Proverbs has been like watching a tight rosebud open gradually day by day into a lush, full, abundant, breathtaking blossom. And blessing upon blessing, each time I read through the 31 chapters in Proverbs, I find more wisdom to help me with my daily challenges and the decisions I must make.

Each day I wanted—and was receiving—what Proverbs 1:2-6 promised: I wanted "to know wisdom and instruction, to discern the sayings of understanding, to receive instruction in wise behavior, righteousness, justice and equity."

- I needed the Word of God to give "prudence to the naive," to give me, a new Christian, "knowledge and discretion."

- I yearned to be the wise person who "will hear and will

> increase in learning," the wise person "of understanding" who "will acquire wise counsel," the wise person who will "understand a proverb and a figure, the words of the wise and their riddles."

Still to this day, each time as I approach my proverb for the day, I can't help but think of these words—which have become a prayer from my heart:

> A truly wise man is not one who has attained,
> but who knows that he has not attained
> and is still pressing onward to perfection.[1]

As a woman after God's own heart I'm sure you too long for these same blessings. So let's start at the very beginning, right here and right now, with Proverbs 1. Let's embrace the Proverbs. Let's pause and ask God to help us gain an understanding heart and a soul filled with wisdom that will better our every day.

The Heart and Soul of Wisdom

Wisdom has its source in God—"For the LORD gives wisdom; from His mouth come knowledge and understanding" (Proverbs 2:6).

Everything has a source. Everything has to start somewhere. Some years ago our family vacationed in the state of Montana. Montana is a *very* large state, and believe me when I say we did a l-o-t of driving. On one memorable morning, we drove over a short bridge with a sign that read "Missouri River"—which caused one of those "Wait a minute!" moments. Our family had been to St. Louis, Missouri, and we had seen the impressive width of the Missouri River just before it empties into the mighty Mississippi. This river in Montana was minute—little more than a rivulet of water—when compared to what we had witnessed in St. Louis. So Jim backed up our Volkswagen camper to make certain we hadn't misread the sign. Sure enough, it was the beginnings of the Missouri River, and we were not very far from its source.

As we think about the nature of God, we need to remember this one important truth: Everything has a source—*except* God. God *is* the source of all things. The heavens and earth have their source in God. All humans—including you—have their beginnings in God. And wisdom has its origin in God: God *is* wisdom, and His wisdom and knowledge are derived from no one because all true wisdom has its source in God.[2]

Wisdom is more than knowledge—"How blessed is the man who finds wisdom and the man who gains understanding" (Proverbs 3:13)!

You can thank God that understanding the wisdom recorded in Proverbs requires no formal education. That's because wisdom is the ability to think clearly and make wise decisions, even (and definitely for a busy woman, wife, mom, and hard worker!) when under pressure and in the midst of difficult situations and the emergencies of life. This, my dear friend, is the kind of wisdom we need to shoulder an unbelievable load of responsibilities and stress each and every day.

Wisdom is available and freely given—Proverbs 1 makes it abundantly clear that God wants His people to be wise and safe (verses 2 and 33). In fact, God has made sure that wisdom is readily available to any and all. It is right in the Bible—*your* Bible—available to you day by day. As Proverbs 3:13 marvels, "How blessed is the man who finds wisdom."

Wisdom comes in a variety of ways—While the Missouri River has one source, it has many tributaries that add to its size and power as it flows toward its destination. The same is true with God's wisdom:

- You gain wisdom by walking with God. The foundation of wisdom is to know and recognize that "the fear of the LORD is the beginning of knowledge" (Proverbs 1:7). As you honor and esteem God, live in awe of His presence and power, make the choices He advises in His Word, and love Him with all your heart, soul, mind, and strength, His wisdom becomes your wisdom. It's yours as you "fear" the Lord—as you walk with Him, honor Him, live for Him, and follow Him wholeheartedly. You exchange your will for His wisdom.

- You gain wisdom from reading God's Word. Reading the Bible can make you wise—wiser than your enemies, your teachers, even those older and more experienced than you. Love God's Word! Hold it first in your heart and mind, and obey it.[3]

For your busy, challenging days, going through a devotional study like this one will help you get into the Bible—and get more out of the Bible. As you gain wisdom from God's Word, it will make a powerful difference in you, in your life—and in your day.

- You gain wisdom from being with God's people. Going to church and worshipping God starts your week with a solid focus. As you fellowship with others, you realize they have wisdom to share with you. In Proverbs 1:5 as we have already noted, "A wise man will hear and increase in learning, and a man of understanding will acquire wise counsel." As a key principle in Proverbs 12:15 states, "The way of a fool is right in his own eyes, but a wise man is he who listens to counsel."

- You can also gain wisdom through having godly mentors and teachers. Watch their lives. Ask them questions and read the wise advice of others through Christian books. In both cases, you are learning and growing as you seek the wisdom of other believers.

God's Wisdom...for Your Day

As you daily make your way through Proverbs, starting in chapter 1, you can't miss the truth that evil does its worst in secret and solicits new followers in the dark. But God's wisdom is public. It's in your face, so to speak. You can't miss it! It's available right in the town square. In fact, it can't be avoided because as verses 20 and 21 note, "Wisdom shouts in the street, she lifts her voice in the square; at the head of the noisy streets she cries out; at the entrance of the gates in the city she utters her sayings."

What problems or trials are you experiencing today? This week? This month? Are you struggling with your roles and responsibilities? Are you at a crossroad in your career? Do you need direction in dealing with a family member, a friend, a workmate, or your finances? Or are you needing some help with all of the above? Then you need wisdom—God's wisdom.

Well, wait no longer! God promises you wisdom—and it's free and readily available. Your job is to pray, seek, search, and dig for God's wisdom in His Word. God's job—and His promise to you—is to give you all the wisdom you ask for...and all the wisdom you need.[4]

Do you realize what this means? It means that whatever issue or problem you are facing, you don't have to grope around in the dark, hoping you will somehow stumble upon answers. You don't have to stab at a solution and hope you made the right choice—the wise choice, all the time fearing that maybe you made the wrong choice. No, you have a surer way to tackle life's problems—and gain God's peace of mind in the process!

Whenever you need wisdom, you can pray to God, ask of God, look to God's Word...and wisdom will be given to you!

And here's another incredible blessing you can expect when you daily seek God's wisdom. It's one of my favorites as a woman. There is so much to tend to, worry about, fear, and beware of. Every minute of every day can be full of fear and charged with anxiety. But this proverb quells all our fears. It's a truth and a promise:

> *But whoever listens to me [wisdom] will dwell safely, and will be secure, without fear of evil.*
> (Proverbs 1:33 NKJV)

2

Parenting with Passion —Childraising—

My son, if you will receive my words
and treasure my commandments within you,
make your ear attentive to wisdom,
incline your heart to understanding...
then you will discern the fear of the Lord
and discover the knowledge of God.

PROVERBS 2:1,2,5

A Prayer to Pray—

Lord, as I read these verses, I am struck by the impassioned words of a parent instructing his child. Then I realize and acknowledge that You, my heavenly Father, are pleading with me and calling me to be a woman who seeks Your divine wisdom through Your Word. Today I want to be more attentive to Your wisdom. I am purposing to incline my heart to a greater understanding of Your majesty, Your will, and Your ways. Open my eyes—and my heart—that I may better comprehend how to worship You and discover more about You, dear Lord—much more! Amen, and amen.

I could not believe it. It was Friday, and my friends had a fun-filled evening all worked out. But my father spoiled everything when he vetoed my plans to go out with my friends that night. I was red-faced embarrassed when I had to call and tell my best friend to let the others know that I couldn't go with them. I knew I would be the laughingstock of my group for weeks to come! Needless to say, I had a tearful evening with my head deeply planted in my pillow.

Do you remember what life was like when you were 16? Friends and cliques (and boys!) were the center of your universe. So I was ecstatic when a group of popular girls asked me to be part of their Friday night activities.

Believe me, I was not looking forward to going to school on Monday. I wanted to stay home, but my dad personally drove me to school. Head down, I walked up the steps to my high school feeling like I was on the way to the gallows—only to get the surprise of my life. It seems my little fun group of girls had been picked up by the police after driving away from the A&W root beer and burger drive-in with the car tray and the glass root beer mugs! All of the girls' parents had to go to the police station and pick up their daughters. I probably don't even need to say this, but—wow, I was soooo glad my dad said no to me that night!

As you can well imagine, my respect and willingness to listen to my dad (and mom too) shot through the roof. He was smarter than I ever guessed! And that wasn't the last time his wisdom bailed me out of tough decisions and gave me direction.

...and life goes on! Ten years later, I was a parent who, along with my husband, was responsible for two little girls. Somehow the wisdom gene had not been passed on to me, and I didn't have a clue about how to raise children...or even how to live my own life! But thankfully, God's Word came to the rescue as I began reading one chapter of Proverbs every day.

Parenting 101

Although God's childraising instructions appear in just about every chapter of Proverbs. Chapter 2 is literally filled with solid, godly direction for parents. Every single verse contains messages, warnings, and instructions for parents to pass on to their children. This wisdom is meant to prepare each child for facing life and avoiding its pitfalls. How does Proverbs say this is done?

As a parent you must speak up. "Receive my words and treasure my commandments within you" and "heed instruction and be wise" (Proverbs 2:1; 8:33). I have read these words so many times that they have become embedded in my heart and thoughts. With passion and a fierce love for God and for our children, parents must speak up! "Wisdom" is portrayed as a woman—a very verbal and vocal woman who is not ashamed or shy about speaking up. She "shouts in the street, she lifts her voice in the square" (1:20). There is nothing casual or half-hearted about her zeal for others to be wise. And for our children, the teaching of wisdom should be even more passionate.

Ideally, instructing and warning your children is to come from both parents. If this is not happening in your family, then you, dear mom, must roll up your mothering sleeves and teach and train your children in the ways of the Lord. This may make instructing your precious kids more difficult, but it definitely makes it more important—vital, in fact—because if in this case Mom doesn't instruct and guide her brood, then no one is likely to do it.

In spite of your situation, never give up. Wisdom is a necessity for your children's lives and well-being. As a wise parent, commit to this responsibility. Own it. Dedicate yourself to be faithful to what God is calling you to do as a parent. And pray for God's guidance. Put this at the top of your daily prayer list: "Lord, please help me to be on my toes today with my children. Help me to speak up and take every opportunity to share Your truths with them."

As we are faithful to follow God's instructions to us as mothers to teach His wisdom to our children, He will faithfully enable us to do it. Lean on Him. Talk to Him. Trust in Him. Desire to be a mom after God's own heart—a mother who will do all God's will, including teaching wisdom to your precious ones.

I love these words written by a devoted father to his two teenage sons. Summing up the benefits of obtaining wisdom and responding to God's call to be wise, he writes:

> [Proverbs] pronounces a blessing on those who heed her instruction, walking in her ways. It promises happiness to those who wait ardently at her gate, who keep faithful vigil at her doors. It holds out life and divine favor to those who find her, but personal loss and death to those who miss her.[1]

Blessing. Happiness. Life and divine favor. This is what we moms want for our children—what we speak up for, what we live for...and what we would die for.

As a parent you must watch over your children. Not only are you to speak up, but you are to look out and watch over your family. I have scores of favorite proverbs that I recite to myself daily as I go through yet another crazy, challenging day. Proverbs 31:27 is one of those because it describes the heart of an excellent wife, mother, and home manager: "She looks well to the ways of her household" (Proverbs 31:27). Another translation I really like simply says, "She keeps watch over all that goes on in her house" (KNOX).

The image of a watchman was a familiar daily occurrence in the days when the book of Proverbs was written. It is also a major theme in the early chapters of Proverbs—that a parent's role is one of watching and warning. The actual picture of the woman who watches over the household affairs is of a woman who has eyes in the back of her head! She looks everywhere so that she doesn't miss a single detail.[2]

A quick overview of the role of a watchman points us to Ezekiel, a major prophet of the Old Testament. God appointed him to be a watchman over His people, saying to Ezekiel, "I have appointed you a watchman for the house of Israel; so you will hear a message from My mouth and give them warning from Me" (Ezekiel 33:7).

God told Ezekiel what he as a watchman was to do when he saw the enemy: He was to blow the trumpet and warn the people. If the people heard God's warning delivered through the prophet but chose not to respond, then the people would be responsible for the consequences of their indifference (verses 3-4).

Then God warned Ezekiel, "But if the watchman sees the sword coming and does not blow the trumpet, and the people are not warned...his blood [the blood of the unprepared people] I will require from the watchman's hand" (verse 6). In other words, if the watchman failed to warn the people, the watchman was held accountable and paid for his failure to warn the people with his own life.

As a parent, you, like Ezekiel, are to *watch* over your family, *listen* to what God says in His Word, and *pass it on* to your children. What should you watch for?

What's going on in their life right now? If something new has taken place (like a new school and a new home in a new city), how is it affecting your child?
Who are their friends, and how well do you know them?
Are you witnessing negative changes in their attitudes and moods?
Are there signs of rebellion toward you or your parental authority?
Are there changes in their appearance or the clothes they are choosing to wear?
Has their attitude about spiritual things changed?

If you have a garden you probably check on your plants, vegetables, fruit, or flowers, every day. If they need water, plant food, or pruning, you take care of the need. Like caring for your garden, watching over your children and warning them takes time. It requires daily attention and action. Being a passionate parent requires stopping what you're doing and devoting time and attention to your children. Don't allow your life and your days to become so busy you neglect instructing and pointing your children toward God and His ways. Waiting increases the possibility that the walls of your child's heart can be breached by the enemy. Don't let down your guard as a watchman. Speak up and do something—now!

God's Wisdom...for Your Day

And here's a challenge and word of encouragement for all women: Give your children the gift of a more problem-free life. You do this by giving them God's truth and wisdom that will keep them from trouble today and in the future. Give them the discernment they need to stay away from those who are evil, who delight in evil, and desire to entice your precious lambs to sin.

The best way for you to teach this to your children is to personally apply and model the wisdom of Proverbs. Are you meeting with God and listening to His voice of wisdom each day? Are you heeding and following His instructions? His counsel? His warnings? Are you hiding the truths of His wisdom in your heart? First and foremost, *be* a woman of wisdom. Then, if you have children, be sure you speak up when correction is needed, and daily point them to God's wisdom. Then, Lord willing, as Proverbs 2:11-12 says, "discretion" will guard your children and "understanding" will watch over them, to deliver them from "the way of evil." Simply put, "Truth is the protector from all evil."[3]

Today, protect yourself from evil by living according to wisdom. Then throw that same protective cloak of wisdom over your children.

3

Finding Peace in a World of Chaos —Trusting God—

Her ways are pleasant ways
and all her paths are peace.
PROVERBS 3:17

A Prayer to Pray—

Dear Father of all comfort, it would be so easy to slide into despair over so many worries like my health, my family, my work, my future, and my country. But Father, because of my relationship with Your Son, the "Prince of Peace," I can experience supernatural peace of heart, soul, and mind in spite of my circumstances. May Your peace that resides in me also be a source of peace and comfort in my home and to those I am in contact with today. Amen.

I've often thought about writing a book entitled *Life Without a Cell Phone*. However, I'm not sure anyone would purchase a book on this topic. Just look around when you're out in a crowd or in a restaurant—even in church! It looks like everyone is either facedown with their faces aglow, reading their messages, scrolling through social media sites, thumbing in text and email messages, scanning through their photos, or, as one of my sons-in-law often does, looking up information on Wikipedia.

Maybe that's why my husband, Jim, and I love our home-sweet-home on the Olympic Peninsula in Washington State. We are five miles from a tiny town with its one stoplight. Except for a variety of bird sounds and the lapping of water, there is silence for most of the day and night. And...there is no cell service! I don't know how this sounds to you, but for writers like Jim and me, who need hours of undistracted focus, our little cabin in the woods is heaven on earth!

So when I came to chapter 3 of Proverbs, my heart leaped with delight because this chapter majors on wisdom that leads to a lifestyle marked by peace. Chapter 3 falls into a long section of nine chapters which focuses on learning the value of wisdom and teaching our children and others so they can enjoy fruitful, successful, and peaceful lives.

Without the knowledge and guidance of God's wisdom, a person's insights will be distorted, and their choices and conclusions will be skewed, and as a result, they will end up making wrong decisions and getting into all sorts of trouble! True insight—true wisdom—comes only from God. As we already know, "the fear of the LORD is the beginning of knowledge" and "the LORD gives wisdom; from His mouth come knowledge and understanding" (Proverbs 1:7; 2:6). A person who has

God's wisdom and understanding will also have God's peace as a by-product.

To pass on what we know of wisdom and knowledge so that other people and our children can experience God's peace, we must first teach them about the God behind that wisdom, the God who "by wisdom founded the earth, by understanding He established the heavens" (Proverbs 3:19). Proverbs 1 introduced us to the wisdom of God. Proverbs 2 emphasized the moral stability that comes with God's wisdom and the ability to discern good from evil, which results in following God's path of wisdom.

God's Wisdom Brings You Peace

And now in chapter 3 the author shows how wisdom promotes peace and serenity. You can have peace...

...by obeying Scripture (Proverbs 3:1)—"My son, do not forget my teaching, but let your heart keep my commandments." Like all good parents and teachers, Wisdom wants the best for her children. She knows that the best comes only through obedience to sound teaching.

...by applying God's Word (Proverbs 3:3-4)—"Do not let kindness and truth leave you; bind them around your neck, write them on the tablet of your heart. So you will find favor and good repute in the sight of God and man." The person who is serious about their outward behavior will "bind" kindness and truth around their neck. To insure that they don't lapse inwardly, they memorize Scripture—they write God's Word on "the tablet" of their heart. Memorizing God's Word then leads to obeying God's Word, and thus obtaining "favor and good repute"

with God and man alike. In other words, obedience leads to a life of peace and harmony.

...by trusting God completely (Proverbs 3:5-6)—"Trust in the LORD with all your heart and do not lean on your own understanding. In all your ways acknowledge Him, and He will make your paths straight." Trusting God is the central element to developing a heart of peace. When a person is rooted in obedience to sound teaching, they will more readily want to trust God for all areas of their life. As a result, "He will make your paths straight." There is no greater peace than knowing you are on the right path.

...by trusting God with your money (Proverbs 3:9-10)—"Honor the LORD from your wealth and from the first of all your produce. So your barns will be filled with plenty and your vats will overflow with new wine." We are stewards who are responsible for the management of God's resources. It is our privilege to use what He gives us to work for the furtherance of His kingdom. When we know and accept that all that we have is God's, we can hold all things lightly because we are holding onto God tightly. Whether the stock market goes up or down or times are tough and money is scarce, we can enjoy complete peace because our treasure is in heaven.

...by welcoming God's discipline (Proverbs 3:11-12)—"My son, do not reject the discipline of the LORD or loathe His reproof, for whom the LORD loves He reproves, even as a father corrects the son in whom he delights." When you and I submit to God's discipline, we will have assurance and peace of mind as we acknowledge that God has a purpose. Coming from an all-knowing Father and loving God, we can be assured that whatever

discipline we receive is for our good and His glory. Discipline is a proof of God's love, and correction is a proof of our sonship.[1]

...by treasuring wisdom (Proverbs 3:13-18)—Wisdom "is more precious than jewels; and nothing you desire compares with her." The blessings won through obtaining wisdom are better than silver and gold, jewels, and anything else you desire. One invaluable prize for seeking and finding wisdom is peace: "Her ways are pleasant ways and all her paths are peace...and happy are all who hold her fast" (verses 17-18).

...by reviewing God's Word constantly (Proverbs 3:21-26)—To further impress upon us the importance of constantly reviewing her teachings, Wisdom cries out once more:

> *My son, let them not vanish from your sight;*
> *keep sound wisdom and discretion,*
> *so they will be life to your soul*
> *and adornment to your neck.*
> (Proverbs 3:21-22)

Earlier I mentioned that wisdom is a lot like common sense or "discretion." Common sense is the ability God gives to all people to think and make good choices. Wisdom, however, is something God gives only to those who follow Him, and it is perfected through knowledge received from instruction, training, and discipline.[2] When you constantly review God's Word and follow His path of wisdom and discretion, you will walk securely, sleep soundly, and experience God's peace in every facet of your stress-filled life.

Note the many promises in the beautiful, reassuring verses that follow. They read like a blessing from God to you, a benediction over your day…and your life. Let them encourage your heart and give you peace.

> *Then you will walk in your way securely*
> *and your foot will not stumble.*
> *When you lie down, you will not be afraid;*
> *When you lie down, your sleep will be sweet.*
> *Do not be afraid of sudden fear*
> *nor of the onslaught of the wicked when it comes;*
> *for the LORD will be your confidence*
> *and will keep your foot from being caught.*
> (Proverbs 3:23-26)

…*by practicing integrity continually* (Proverbs 3:27-32)—It's sad but true that we often experience conflicts with others for doing what is right. This last section begins with five "Do nots" that tell us what not to do so that we live with integrity.

What does a person with integrity look like? It is a person who consistently walks with God, and…

> will not be selfish,
> will not be stingy,
> will not be plotting evil,
> will not be argumentative and contentious, and
> will not be envious of evil (verses 27-31).

Yes, you and I may be hassled by others for always desiring to do what is right. But when we do what is right, we never have to worry about our actions before God. We can end each day with peace of mind knowing that we have honored God that day by living with integrity.

In the Old Testament, Daniel was just such a person. When evil men tried to find some reason to condemn him before the king, Daniel 6:4 says, "They could find no ground of accusation or evidence of corruption, inasmuch as he was faithful, and no negligence or corruption was to be found in him." It's no wonder God's angel referred to Daniel twice as "O man of high esteem" in Daniel 10.

This is how God views integrity—and these words paint a picture of what integrity looks like and stands for. Surely this quality should be our goal as well!

God's Wisdom...for Your Day

As a Christian you already know that Jesus Christ gives you "positional peace"—a peace that comes from knowing God through His Son. Proverbs 3, however, speaks of the peace that comes as you live according to God's practical wisdom like that which makes up the book of Proverbs. In just this one chapter, Proverbs teaches you that peace is the result of these practices:

...obeying Scripture

...applying God's Word

...trusting God completely

...trusting God with your money

...welcoming God's discipline

...treasuring God's wisdom

...reviewing God's Word constantly

...practicing godly integrity continually

As you face this day's joys and sorrows, its challenges and delights, single out the practice in the above list that will help you navigate your day with a peace that passes all understanding—a peace that can only come from the Prince of Peace. As Paul prayed, "Now the God of peace be with you all. Amen" (Romans 15:33).

4

Guarding Your Heart
—Watchfulness—

Watch over your heart with all diligence,
for from it flow the springs of life.
PROVERBS 4:23

A Prayer to Pray—

O Father, I thank You that You watch over me, Your grateful child, with utmost care. May I also be careful to watch over my ways and my heart, and follow You all the days of my life. It is the desire of my heart to put away all excuses and laziness, and faithfully tend to my heart's condition and hold Your Word fast in my heart. Amen.

One thing I love about Proverbs 4 is we have the opportunity to meet a family in which three generations have run the race of raising their children. The writer links together three generations—his father, himself, and now his son (verses 1,3). He demonstrates how a love of the best things ("sound teaching"—verse 2) will be transmitted mainly by personal influence over many years. Two lifetimes had already been spent in this training (the grandfather and the father), and now a third generation is to take up the challenge to live a godly life of wisdom.

Getting to the Heart of the Matter

Proverb 4 makes it clear that the heart is the focal point for all your actions and behavior. Therefore you and I must "watch over your heart with all diligence, for from it flow the springs of life" (verse 23).

The heart is a popular topic both in and out of the Bible. The word "heart" appears over 800 times in the Bible. The book of Psalms has the most references to the heart (127 times), but the book of Proverbs, which is much shorter, is second with 69 references. As you can see, the heart is a key subject in Proverbs.

Why would Proverbs and God, its ultimate author, fixate on the heart? Here's one definition that helps explain how the Hebrews thought of "the heart":

> ...it was essentially the whole man, with all his attributes, physical, intellectual, and psychological...The heart was conceived of as the governing center of all of these...It is the heart which governs all actions, character, personality, will, and mind.[1]

We could say the heart is a person's control center. This applies to our actions and attitudes. They are a reflection of our hearts. Proverbs 4:23 says that the heart—our governing center—is the focal point of our behavior: "From it flows the spring of life." All that we do, say, and think is an expression of the overflow and the condition of the heart. Therefore the watch-care of our heart cannot be a casual thing.

And not just watch-care, but diligent watch-care: "Watch over your heart with all diligence." Diligence has the idea of posting a guard on constant duty. Diligence involves and requires steady, earnest, energetic effort 24/7/365—all day, every day for life.

Here are just a few of the many proverbs about the heart that appear in only the first four chapters of Proverbs. They provide motivation and instruction for your heart, on the importance of your heart, and on your care of your heart.

> *Make your ear attentive to wisdom,*
> *incline your heart to understanding* (2:2).
>
> *For wisdom will enter your heart*
> *and knowledge will be pleasant to your soul* (2:10).
>
> *My son, do not forget my teaching,*
> *but let your heart keep my commandments* (3:1).
>
> *Do not let kindness and truth leave you;*
> *bind them around your neck,*
> *write them on the tablet of your heart* (3:3).
>
> *Trust in the Lord with all your heart;*
> *and do not lean on your own understanding* (3:5).
>
> *Then he taught me and said to me,*
> *"Let your heart hold fast my words"* (4:4).

Learning from Past Generations

Let's eavesdrop on the kind of teaching the three generations seen in Proverbs 4 taught and received. We are privileged to listen in on this heart-to-heart talk prompted by love and passionate care. In Proverbs 4, we receive three admonitions:

Admonition #1—"Give attention" (Proverbs 4:1).

"Attention" is the capacity to maintain concentration on something. The father's immediate concern is that his child focus full attention on his father's teaching. Attention is necessary in the acquisition of understanding, of getting wisdom, and receiving instruction. If this had been a military situation, the leader would have said, "Listen up!" Or as you hear so many moms say to their kids, "Are you listening to me?"

Like the father in Proverbs 4, our heavenly Father offers us, His children, "sound teaching." He is pleading with us: "Do not abandon my instruction...Do not forget nor turn away from the words of my mouth. Do not forsake her" (verses 2,5-6). Holding fast to His words, which are words of wisdom, will provide these benefits:

> They will promote life (verse 4).
> They will guard and watch over you (verse 6).
> They will give you understanding (verse 7).
> They will exalt and honor you (verse 8).

Admonition #2—"Accept my sayings" (Proverbs 4:10-19).

I'm sure you've heard the saying, "You can lead a horse to water, but you can't make it drink." It is only when the horse gets thirsty enough that it will take a drink. The word "accept" has the idea of "taking away" instruction. It's like a takeaway truth. We are to listen (verse 1) and then snatch up God's teachings and carry them away in our hearts.

In Proverbs 4:10-19, two paths are set before us in a comparison:

> Path one—Verses 10-13 describes this path as the "way of wisdom," as the "upright paths." Verse 18 paints this beautiful word picture: "The path of the righteous is like the light of dawn, that shines brighter and brighter until the full day" (verse 18).
>
> Path two—Verses 14-17 refer to this option as "the path of the wicked," the "way of evil men." In contrast to the brilliance of verse 18, the writer explains, "The way of the wicked is like darkness; they do not know over what they stumble" (verse 19).

It's almost as if we hear the writer's appeal: "Will you choose the light, or will you choose the darkness? Will you choose the way of wisdom, or will you choose the way of the wicked?"

Admonition #3—"Incline your ear" (Proverbs 4:20-27).

Think about your own life and your journey in spiritual growth. Do you immediately respond to everything you read in Scripture, or to every sermon your pastor preaches? If you do, then you are highly unusual. However, most people have a very short attention span. Godly change doesn't happen overnight. The major part of godliness comes from hearing familiar truths over and over—and over!—again, repeated enough times until it finally sinks in. Then we start all over again and take another step toward godliness.

In this section of Proverbs 4 you will encounter constant repetition. We are called to watch over all aspects of our life, which are symbolized by the mouth, eyes, and feet.

The mouth (verse 24)—After our thoughts (which come from the heart), come our words. That's what Jesus said in Matthew 12:34: "For out of the abundance of the heart the mouth speaks."

The heart is where words originate, but actions, like deceit and devious lips, are only a symptom of a heart condition. We must deal with both the source and the symptom.

The eyes (verse 25)—Someone has said, "The eyes are the gateway to the soul" (author unknown). Most sin starts with the eyes. King David was a prime example. The first act that later led to adultery and murder started with his eyes: "He saw a woman bathing; and the woman was very beautiful in appearance" (2 Samuel 11:2).

Proverbs 4:25 warns us not to let our eyes stray. We are told, "Let your eyes look directly ahead...straight in front of you." That's good advice for all of us for all time!

The feet (verses 26-27)—The next warning is about the feet: "Watch the path of your feet...Do not turn to the right nor to the left." Another translation says "ponder the path of your feet" (NKJV). This verse is prescribing the idea of weighing one's course of action before proceeding. Or as I'm sure you've heard it said: "Look before you leap!"

God's Wisdom...for Your Day

How is your heart condition? Millions of people check their blood pressure every day to keep tabs on their heart. You, too, must keep a close eye on your heart as you grow in Christ. Tend to your heart daily. Guard your heart by putting away sin and putting on the righteousness of Christ. When you do this, your heart will be centered on Christ. As our verse for this chapter urges, "Watch over your heart with all diligence, for from it flow the springs of life."

Be encouraged, my friend. And praise God, you are never alone. God is always there, "a very present help in trouble" (Psalm 46:1). The Holy Spirit comes alongside you to encourage you daily as you gain and apply the wisdom of Proverbs.

5

Being a Faithful Wife
—Marriage—

May your fountain be blessed,
and may you rejoice in the wife of your youth...
may you ever be intoxicated with her love.

PROVERBS 5:18-19 NIV

A Prayer to Pray—

Dear Father in heaven, as a faithful, covenant-keeping God, You have not abandoned Your people in the past, nor will You abandon Your relationship with me in the present. Help me to be steadfast and faithful in the marriage covenant I have made with my husband. Forsaking all others, may I daily strive to be a loving wife after Your own heart. Amen.

It's no surprise that marriage as an institution has definitely fallen on hard times. The secular world seems to have given up on marriage. The world says marriage doesn't work and is not necessary, so why should a couple go through a ceremony? Why not simply live together?

Yet marriage was the first institution God ordained when He brought the first man and woman together with this benediction: "For this reason a man shall leave his father and his mother, and be joined to his wife; and they shall become one flesh" (Genesis 2:24). This one verse tells us:

- God instituted marriage.
- Marriage is to be monogamous and heterosexual.
- Marriage partners are to become one flesh and enjoy an intimate physical union.

In addition, Jesus taught that marriage is to be permanent (see Mark 10:7-9).

Throughout the book of Proverbs, and especially Proverbs 5, we find instructions to two specific groups of readers.

God's Instructions to Wives

When you read the beautiful, poetic words in Proverbs 5:18-19, you can't help but admire the loving role God expects a wife to have in her husband's life.

- She is to be a fountain of blessing to him.
- She is to bring her husband such joy that he rejoices at his good fortune to have found her.

- She is to be like a tender, loving deer and a lovely and graceful doe.

- She is to relish her role of pleasing and satisfying her husband.

Because of her consuming love for him, her husband is always infatuated, intoxicated, lost in, and drunk on her love. As the saying goes, he thinks she hung the moon!

This type of deep-seated daily love and loyalty is modeled by the excellent wife throughout Proverbs 31: "The heart of her husband trusts in her, and he will have no lack of gain." Why? Because "she does him good and not evil all the days of her life" (verses 11-12).

This picture of a faithful wife is the key to what the dad is about to teach his son in Proverbs 5. Through this wise father, God Himself is saying that a marriage that honors God and fulfills His intentions for a married couple will go a long way in providing a model not only for their children, but also for the world of God's perfect and pure design for marriage.

The devil, who is "a liar and the father of lies" (John 8:44), would like nothing better than to destroy God's plan for marriages and family. He works relentlessly to lure marriage partners away from one another and their vows and into a life of adultery and promiscuity. Needless to say, if you are married, you can and must do your part to be faithful to your husband in your thoughts, conduct, and actions.

God's Instructions to Children

The book of Proverbs makes it clear that youth and young adults must be instructed to remain sexually pure. In Proverbs 5 a wise father is once again teaching and warning his son about the evil and immoral woman, the seductress, all of which apply to you and your marriage. This instruction will be repeated and reinforced throughout the remainder of the book of Proverbs. This gives us a pretty good idea of how important sexual purity is to God and should be to us and to our children!

Think about it. How many times have you repeated something vitally important over and over to your children? For instance, did you ever tell your preschooler, "Don't play in the street"? And did you only tell them once? Oh no, you told them every single time they went out to play! Their life depended on your instruction—and their obedience.

As every good teacher—and caring parent—knows, repetition is the key to learning! The father and parent in Proverbs 5 is no different. Because he is wise, and because he cares, and because the information is vital to his child's future, this faithful, passionate parent is going to continue his instruction.

It would be incredible if your husband would take on this role. But if he is not at home due to his job or his work schedule, then you as your beloved child's parent will need to drill this same information into your children's hearts. And you can't have this talk just once and mark it off your "Things Good Parents Do" list. You must do it over and over...and over again. Proverbs 5 gives you a list of topics to cover.

#1: Beware of the seductress (Proverbs 5:1-6). One reason some parents dread the teen years is having to prepare their children to handle boy/girl relationships. And the father of Proverbs 5 is no different. This devoted parent begins by painting a graphic picture of a woman his son and all men should be aware of and recognize as an adulteress and avoid completely. How can a man recognize a seductress?

- Her words are devious (Proverbs 5:3)—"The lips of an adulteress drip honey and smoother than oil is her speech."

- Her charm is deceitful (Proverbs 5:4)—All the charming words and actions of an adulteress are a lie. In reality "she is bitter as [poisonous] wormwood, sharp as a two-edged sword."

- Her ultimate end is death (Proverbs 5:5-6)—This woman's steps lead to death, and those who associate with her meet a similar fate. Rather than choosing life, she chooses death and gladly takes an unsuspecting young man down with her!

#2: Unfaithfulness pays a high price (Proverbs 5:7-14). We love to praise God and rejoice in His grace and forgiveness. However, there is always a consequence to our sin. In childraising there are two approaches to teaching and impressing our children. One is to tell them the many good things that happen and result from doing what's right, from making the right choices. The other is to vividly, bluntly, and accurately describe the results and disastrous consequences that come when a choice is made to do what is wrong.

As difficult as it may be to speak up, to talk frankly, to warn his children and describe the cost of giving in to adultery, this father goes on in verses 7-8: "Now then, my sons, listen to me and do not depart from the words of my mouth. Keep your way far from her and do not go near the door of her house." Then he lays out five consequences of unfaithfulness in a marriage. Any one of these should make a listener and reader think twice before having an illicit relationship.

- A wasted life (verse 9): You "give your vigor to others."

- Financial loss (verse 10): Strangers "feast on your wealth and your toil enrich[es] the house of another" (NIV).
- Mental anguish (verse 11): "...and you groan at your final end, when your flesh and your body are consumed."
- Self-reproach (verses 12-13): "...and you say, 'How I have hated instruction! And my heart spurned reproof! I have not listened to the voice of my teachers, nor inclined my ear to my instructors!'"
- Public ruin (verse 14): "I was almost in utter ruin in the midst of the assembly and congregation."

These consequences of unfaithfulness are drastic and alarming and shocking. Yet the faithful father doesn't stop with shock value. He instead describes the better—and best—choice. Using the imagery of water, he contrasts the disaster of infidelity with the refreshing joy and abundant life a faithful marriage brings to both partners and their children. He warns his son to "drink water from your own cistern and fresh water from your own well" instead of letting his water run in the streets (verses 15-16).

#3: Faithfulness reaps blessings upon blessings (Proverbs 5:15-20). In these verses, the father argues why a man should be faithful to his wife: His marriage offers everything!—and the lure of the world and an adulteress offers nothing. He ends this man-to-man talk in verse 20 with this rhetorical question: "Why should you, my son, be exhilarated with an adulteress?" If we were asking this question today, we might say, "Why in the world would you ever even look at an adulteress when you've got a wonderful wife at home?"

#4: Always choose God's way (Proverbs 5:21-23). The bottom line for all our actions should be to have God's approval. God is always and ever aware of the choices His children make. "The ways of a man are before the eyes of the LORD, and He watches all his paths" (verse 21). If you are married, fidelity and faithfulness to your spouse is *always* the right path, the better path—there is no other path. You never have to wonder what God wants you to do, for faithfulness in marriage is *God's* path!

God's Wisdom...for Your Day

I have to admit as I sit here with my Bible, reading this impassioned passage in Proverbs 5, I am moved. And I am convicted. Like this father, our Father God loves us so much that he is committed to teach us. He instructs us. He pleads with us. He points out the pitfalls of life. He does everything He can to help us, his beloved, cherished children, avoid sin and evil and the disastrous consequences that are sure to come when His instructions are not heeded.

This chapter's long admonition contrasting marriage and adultery, spoken from the heart of God, is definitely something to apply to ourselves and pass on to our children. What can you do as a seriously concerned, devoted, and passionate wife?

Pray without ceasing. From your child's first breath of life (and even before), through all their growing years and beyond, until your own dying breath, pray for your children. And while you are praying, pray this for yourself:

God, help me to hold on to my vow of marriage. Give me strength to be faithful to You...and to the spouse You give to me. Amen.[1]

Provide a model of a God-centered marriage. You can talk all you want about godliness, purity, and love, but if your children see you and your husband model these qualities, that will make a lasting impression. One picture is worth a thousand words!

Practice what God preaches:

- Stay alert. Be on guard. You live in the world, but you are not of the world. So always prepare your heart before you step into the world.
- Be careful about your own behavior toward men and how you dress.
- Train and teach your children how to resist sin and temptation.
- Love God more than anything in this world.
- Be faithful to God's standards and His will. And, of course,
- Be faithful to your husband. "The heart of her husband trusts in her" (Proverbs 31:11).

6

Following God's Advice
—Character—

My son, observe the commandment of your father
and do not forsake the teaching of your mother;
bind them continually on your heart;
tie them around your neck.
When you walk about, they will guide you;
when you sleep, they will watch over you;
and when you awake, they will talk to you.
For the commandment is a lamp
and the teaching is light.

PROVERBS 6:20-23

A Prayer to Pray—

Dear Lord, I only have one life to offer in Your service. I desire that my life would be a reflection of Your holy character. Search me, O Lord, and know my heart. As Your Word says, You love a heart that is humble and seeks only good for others. Lead me in Your everlasting ways that I may honor You and bless others. Amen.

What Not to Be

One distinguishing quality of a great author is the ability to keep reviewing events and characters in new and creative ways. *A Tale of Two Cities* is a classic novel written by Charles Dickens in 1859. It was set in two cities, London and Paris, before and during the French Revolution. This book has sold more than 200 million copies, and by some estimates is the best-selling novel of all time.

As you read Dickens's book, you can't help but notice that he describes his characters by giving them visual quirks, which he mentions over and over. This is exactly what is happening as we are progressing through the first nine chapters of the book of Proverbs. Its author has certain types of individuals and certain character qualities which he continues to reintroduce in chapter after chapter.

Once again in Proverbs 6 the author speaks as a concerned father. He is giving his son advice. More importantly, he is giving his son God's advice. As you read, note the three new types of people introduced in our growing list of "characters" to watch out for in this true-to-life drama. Especially note the specific advice given.

The person who lends too much (Proverbs 6:1-5). After many warnings about associating with bad company and immoral women, this devoted dad switches to giving financial advice. He warns you and me and all readers against becoming liable for the financial obligations of others saying, "If you have become surety..." (verse 1). This means being a cosigner—the one who is responsible for the debt if the borrower defaults.

Let's put you into this scenario: Suppose a relative or friend wants to buy a car and make loan payments. However, his credit rating is not good enough to finance the purchase, so the car dealer demands the signature of someone who could make the payments if the buyer defaults. The potential buyer—your friend or relative—then comes to you and asks you to cosign the note. If you sign, you "have given a pledge."

What is the best way to handle this kind of request? Take time to think and pray and ask for advice. Don't feel pressured by any kind of time limit. Take all the time you need before you make this kind of commitment. If you are married, your husband should be involved from the first minute. And of course this should be true for him as well.

If you do rush in and decide you have made a mistake, verses 3-5 tell you what to do: You should try to persuade that relative or neighbor to let you out of the promise or vow. This matter is of such importance that you should not even rest until you are released from the liability.

Why does the Bible warn so sternly against becoming surety? Is this some kind of harsh Old Testament law that doesn't show kindness to friends or neighbors? Consider these reasons why you should take your time and be sure before agreeing to cosign for a loan:

- You might be helping someone buy something which is not God's will for them to have.

- You might be discouraging the development of your friend's patience, faith, and trust in God. If God wants them to have it, He will provide it.

- You may be practicing bad stewardship. You are to be a wise and careful steward of what you have. "It is required of stewards that one be found trustworthy" (1 Corinthians 4:2).

- You risk the possibility of bitterness in a close relationship, especially if that person defaults on their loan. It is better for them to be upset with you right away when you say "no" than for you to shoulder the results of a default in the future.

The biblical approach is to discern if there is a real and legitimate need. If so, it is better to give money outright, than to become surety.

The person who sleeps too much (Proverbs 6:6-11). I'm sure you've seen a slug crossing a sidewalk. Well, that's the picture of our next person who lacks character—the sluggard.

With the image of a slug in your mind, picture the activity of the ant. These teensy little creatures are diligent and industrious. The focus is not that they are preparing for the future, but on how hard they work.

The lazy person is just the opposite of the industrious ant. He loves his sleep. He loves the snooze button on his alarm. And he loves turning on his hinges over and over on his bed (see Proverbs 26:14). Unfortunately, he will not love the outcome of his indolence. Whatever wealth he might possess or hopes to acquire will be snatched away as if by a thief or a vagrant.

I don't know about you, but I never seem to have enough time. Time is fleeting, and it's something that, when lost, can never be recovered. Every time-management book I have ever read says that the best way to have more time is to "buy time back." How is this done? One way is to become more efficient: Learn to take five minutes to do something that in the past took ten minutes. Another way to buy back time is to do just the opposite of the sluggard and get less sleep…or at least get up when your alarm goes off!

Are you thinking you don't have enough time to read your Bible and pray? Well, problem solved! Get up early enough to read and pray.

Are you thinking you want to learn a new skill, another language? It's been estimated that anyone can become an "expert" on any subject if they will spend just 15 minutes a day on that subject. How can you do this? It's simple: Get up 15 minutes earlier each day and spend that amount of time on your goal until you are an expert!

The person who deceives too much (Proverbs 6:12-19). Do you know what a "con man" is? Well, meet him now. He's the "confidence man," the swindler, as he was described almost 3000 years ago. Here he is called "a worthless person, a wicked man" (verse 12). How is he portrayed?

- His speech is filled with lies.

- His suggestive gestures and deceptive motions signal his accomplices or in some way take his victims off guard.

- His heart is filled with malice and deceit as he constantly plots mischief and discord.

- His doom is certain. He may think he's getting away with his misdeeds, but his sins will find him out, either in this life or the afterlife. He has a terminal illness with no cure.

God has His own lists, and two of them—called "numerical proverbs"—are found here and also in Proverbs 30:15-33. Proverbs 6:16 states, "There are six things which the LORD hates, yes, seven which are an abomination to Him." By using two different numbers, God, the author, indicates that this list is not exhaustive. It's a list of character qualities found in any person God dislikes. God is telling us these attitudes and actions should never be a part of our lives. Here are the seven in verses 16-19:

1. A proud look or "haughty eyes." This look says, "I'm better than you. You are a nobody, whereas I'm a somebody."
2. A lying tongue. Even a half-truth is a lie.
3. A murderous heart. This is a reminder of God's sixth commandment: "You shall not murder" (Exodus 20:13). Jesus took this commandment one step further and said it's not just the act but the thought that makes a person guilty (see Matthew 5:22).
4. A heart that deceives. This is a heart that is always plotting and concocting wicked plans and schemes.
5. Feet that are quick to turn to evil. God hates not only the mind that plans evil, but also the feet that are eager to carry it out!
6. A false witness. God hates those who give a false witness and despises the harm done to those who are falsely accused.

7. A sower of discord. Notice where this action takes place—"among brothers."

God's Wisdom...for Your Day

Wow! Having this list of things God hates right here in front of you should act as a flashing red warning light! May these many negative behaviors God hates serve as daily warnings and instruction. May these pictures and truths from God's Word move you to resolve not to slip up or be lax or lukewarm in desiring—and embracing—God's highest standard for your conduct and character.

As a woman who desires to walk with God day in and day out, you can be confident you are pleasing God when you commit daily to turn the seven "things which the Lord hates...which are an abomination to Him" into these positive and lovely Christlike character qualities. Pray fervently that you will possess:

A humble heart. "Humble yourselves in the presence of the Lord, and He will exalt you" (James 4:10).

A truthful mouth. "Let your statement be, 'Yes, yes' or 'No, no'; anything beyond these is of evil" (Matthew 5:37).

A desire to see others experience eternal life. "And we know that the Son of God has come, and has given us understanding so that we may know Him who is true; and we are in Him who is true, in His Son Jesus Christ. This is the true God and eternal life" (1 John 5:20).

A heart that seeks only good for others. "With good will render service, as to the Lord, and not to men" (Ephesians 6:7).

Feet that are quick to turn from evil. "Now flee from youthful lusts and pursue righteousness, faith, love and peace, with those who call on the Lord from a pure heart" (2 Timothy 2:22).

A mouth that speaks as a faithful witness. "Let no unwholesome word proceed from your mouth, but only such a word as is good for edification according to the need of the moment, so that it will give grace to those who hear" (Ephesians 4:29).

A sower of peace and harmony. "If possible, so far as it depends on you, be at peace with all men" (Romans 12:18).

7

Living a Life of Purity —Morals—

Say to wisdom, "You are my sister,"
and call understanding your intimate friend;
that they may keep you from an adulteress,
from the foreigner who flatters with her words.
PROVERBS 7:4-5

A Prayer to Pray—

Lord, create a clean heart and renew a right spirit in me as I moment by moment strive today to live a life that is wholly acceptable in Your sight. May I meditate through this day and into the night on Your Word so I might present to You a heart of wisdom and a life of purity. Amen.

Do you remember your first impressions of the Bible? For many people, the Bible appears to be a large and imposing volume weighing anywhere up to five pounds! For those who venture into its pages, a casual reading could cause them to think that the tome that is the Bible is filled with material that seems to have little or no significance in our modern world.

But this is in no way true. As the Bible declares, it was written by God. It is God's written declaration of Himself to man. Everything we need to know about God, about life, and about godliness and morals can be found between the covers of this amazing book.

As a result, the Bible does not ramble. God is not merely filling up pages. Every word and every statement in the Bible has meaning, and when something is repeated, God has a reason. One of His often-repeated subjects in Proverbs, chapters 1–6, is the immoral woman. Well, prepare yourself! The entirety of Proverbs 7 deals with this subject. This is no accident, for God makes no mistakes. It is purposeful because a lack of morals is a problem for all people for all of time. This subject is as relevant today as it was 3000 years ago when Proverbs 7 was written.

Since immorality is such a major problem, how can you and I avoid, approach, and manage this rampant problem? How can we stay pure in an impure world? Proverbs 6:20-35 and all of chapter 7 address this issue.

Obeying God's Word Leads to Purity

Here's a great axiom that seems to say it all: "The Bible will keep you from sin, or sin will keep you from the Bible." It is evident as we are introduced to the topic of the adulteress that wording like "observe the commandment" and "keep my words, and treasure my commandments within you" are alerting us to the importance of God's "commandments." Here are some keys to avoiding immorality and living a life of purity:

Observe God's commands (Proverbs 6:20; 7:1-2)—God wants His children to live a moral life according to His Word. He wants us to treat His Word and His commands as profound, serious, and vitally important, and that includes the sin of immorality.

Internalize God's commands (Proverbs 6:21-22; 7:3)—It's one thing to read God's Word, but you reach a whole new level of wisdom when you internalize it. Regarding His Word and His commandments, God instructs us to "bind them continually on your heart" and "write them on the tablet of your heart." Both of these Scriptures are referring to the habit of memorizing God's Word.

When we memorize and meditate on God's Word, it is with us at all times. Wherever you go and whatever temptation comes your way, God's Word in your heart and mind will guide you. When you sleep, it will watch over you. And when you awake, it will speak to you. It's much harder to sin when God's Word is written on your heart and flowing through your mind like blood flows through your body. That's what the psalmist advised in Psalm 119:9,11:

> *How can a young man keep his way pure?*
> *By keeping it according to Your word...*
> *Your word I have treasured in my heart,*
> *that I may not sin against You.*

Trust God's commands to guide you (Proverbs 6:23-24; 7:5)—Life in our fallen world is a murky, precarious, deceptive undertaking. There are myriads of dangers for a child of God. It is extremely reassuring to know that God's Word gives you guidance in the same way a lamp is a light to guide you down a dark path:

> *For the commandment is a lamp,*
> *and the teaching is light.*
> (Proverbs 6:23)

Count on God's commands to guard you (Proverbs 6:24; 7:4-5)—Both Proverbs 6:24 and 7:5 use the word "keep," which conveys the idea of a guard—a bodyguard—keeping watch over you so you are safe. In the same way, God wants to protect you and yours from the evil that surrounds you.

Rejecting God's Word Leads to Sin

The parent and father in Proverbs 6:24-35 carefully describes what an evil adulteress looks like, how she acts, and the tragic consequences to those who reject God's wisdom and choose to have an illicit, immoral relationship. She...

...uses her beauty and speech to seduce her prey. Be careful what you say. Don't use enticing or flirtatious language.

...reduces her prey to poverty. She sucks the life and soul—and money—from those who follow after her.

...destroys both character and reputation. Once a man's character has been ruined, it is almost impossible to reclaim it.

...inflicts a crime that cannot be repaid. A thief can make restitution for his crimes even if it takes all he possesses. An adulterer, however, can never fully erase the damages incurred to all parties—husband, wife, children, and relatives—through adultery. No amount of money would ever be enough to satisfy the violation of a man's marriage, his family, and their reputation.

Rejecting God's Word Leads to Ruin

The temptation to adultery all begins with a seduction (7:6-10). The simpleminded youth is pictured as passing by the harlot's house at "nightfall"—a clear case of choosing to be in the wrong place at the wrong time. In Proverbs 7:10-23 we witness a woman's step-by-step seduction that leads to the act of adultery. Although these instructions are for men to identify and beware of an adulteress, it definitely helps us as women to reject any and all of the ways of an adulteress so we don't tempt men to sin or cause them to stumble with lust. An adulteress:

> Her appearance—The way the adulteress is dressed ("as a harlot"), and
>
> the way she acts ("boisterous and rebellious"), along with her looks ("a brazen face") and
>
> her waywardness ("her feet do not remain at home; she is now in the streets, now in the squares, and lurks by every corner") are dead giveaways as to what she is and what her purpose is.
>
> Her approach—She is bold and brash: "She seizes him and kisses him."
>
> Her provision—Having offered her "peace offerings" to God in the temple, she has a good supply of meat on hand and urges her victim to

come home with her and share it with her since it must be eaten soon.

Her flattery—She pretends that he is "the one" she has been looking for, that he is important.

Her suggestion and invitation—She describes her bed, then gives an open invitation for the night.

Her declaration—She further disarms her male victim by explaining that the man of the house is not at home and won't be back for a long time.

His destruction—Immediately, he follows her, like an animal about to be slaughtered, or a bird about to be snared. He does not realize his decision will cost him his life.

God's Wisdom...for Your Day

Sensuality is alive and thriving in our secular society. Satan is in the business of perverting the bliss and blessing of a fulfilling, monogamous marriage. What can you do today to prepare and protect yourself from this onslaught? How can you put God's wisdom to work in your home and family today?

Create a home that loves God, loves His Word, and commits to follow it. Live your daily life in a way that bears witness that God is real and His Word transforms lives, starting with you and your husband and extending to your children.

Live out God's plan for you as a Christian wife. Do what you must to make sure your marriage is healthy. Again, a picture is worth a thousand words. Your children need to see that marriage is a blessing, one filled with love and respect and commitment—and purity.

8

Leading a Life Marked by Wisdom

—Success—

Blessed is the man who listens to me,
watching daily at my gates,
waiting at my doorposts.
PROVERBS 8:34

A Prayer to Pray—

Dear God of new beginnings, I praise and thank You that in Your infinite wisdom You have given me a guidebook for nurturing wisdom in my life. Help me be faithful to read and study Your book of wisdom—the Bible. I pray, dear Father, that today I will show forth a small portion of that wisdom in the way I speak, act, and live. Then, by Your grace, tomorrow may I be a better testimony of the only wise God, and my Savior, the Lord Jesus Christ. Amen.

In the country of Taiwan, Jim and I were blessed to experience the Bible alive. For years I had been reading Proverbs each and every day...which means for years I had been reading the verse above, Proverbs 8:34: "Blessed is the man who listens to me, watching daily at my gates, waiting at my doorposts." Our family was staying in a mission compound—and experienced the terror—and wonder—of going through a typhoon our first night there! Several days later, after the streets dried up, debris was removed, and electricity was restored, we went on our first outing. Our sponsor had arranged for us and our two preteen daughters to go to a local university to sit and converse with students who were learning English.

There was just one catch. These English lessons were open to anyone and everyone. Those who came didn't have to be enrolled as students in the university. At 5:30 a.m. we went into shock as we neared the gated walls of the university. Thousands of people were crammed around the school's gates that would open at 6:00 a.m. for free English lessons. It was actually a little scary as we were escorted through the crowd and led to a special door by guards so we could set up for the lessons prior to six o'clock.

Truly, I was seeing a verse in the Bible come alive. This scene and experience was a living illustration for me of what it means to value and crave wisdom—to watch daily at Wisdom's gates and to wait at her doorposts and to listen attentively. These dear people desired to learn English so badly they put it as the first thing of the day. They rose in the dark and journeyed to a location hoping to be among the limited number before the cutoff number was reached. I was convicted because this, my sister in Christ, is how we should approach each day—rising early, making any and every sacrifice to read God's Word, to listen to His wisdom, to watch and wait eagerly for every word that proceeds out of His mouth.

Hear Wisdom's Entreaty

Right away in Proverbs 8, verse 1, we learn that "Wisdom" calls from the hilltops and crossroads, telling all who will listen of the importance of accepting her words. Wisdom is using every means available to stir up the people to make a decision in her favor, to choose to be wise, to be careful. Hear her pleading words now. What Wisdom offers is...

Valid (Proverbs 8:1-9)—The wisdom of God is relevant and available.

- "Let me give you discernment and common sense."
- "Everything I say will produce the right results."
- "I speak the truth and hate every kind of deception and perversion."
- "My advice is good and wholesome."
- "My words are simple and plain to anyone with understanding."

Valuable (Proverbs 8:10-11,18-21)—Wisdom is more precious than silver, gold, or rubies. That's what King Solomon believed and why he asked God for "wisdom and knowledge" instead of riches (2 Chronicles 1:11). Those who possess wisdom are equipped to be successful. They will make good use of what they have, they will prosper, and better still, they will be and do good and be honored.

Vital (Proverbs 8:12-17)—All of God's people need wisdom to manage, lead, and judge wisely in their sphere of influence. They must be able to…

give good advice,
have sound judgment,
be understanding,
have their emotions under control,
guide others with righteous judgment, and
possess a learner spirit.

Eternal (Proverbs 8:22-31)—Wisdom is also eternal.

- Wisdom is God's companion from eternity past.
- Wisdom has always existed and has always been a part of God's activities, specifically creation.
- Wisdom is God's constant delight. For a truly devotional experience, read and savor Proverbs 8:22-29.[1]

Rewarding (Proverbs 8:32-36)—Wisdom closes with her final appeal for mankind to accept her: "Now therefore, O sons, listen to me, for blessed are they who keep my ways." God's followers are blessed because:

- Only wisdom will bring abundant life. "For he who finds me finds life." Wisdom is truly more valuable than all the riches in the world. Wealth cannot give life. It may better our life, but only God's wisdom found in Jesus Christ can give life—abundant life, eternal life: "I came that they may have life, and have it abundantly" (John 10:10).

- Only wisdom will gain God's approval. Only the wise "obtains favor from the LORD" (Proverbs 8:35).

Meet a Woman of Wisdom

As I've been reading these opening chapters of Proverbs and seen the many qualities and benefits wisdom produces, it has given me a greater desire for that kind of blessed life. Then I wonder, What would a woman with this kind of wisdom look like?

Mentally turning the pages of my Bible, one woman stands out as a woman of wisdom—a woman who acts and speaks and manages her life with wisdom. She was not a national leader in her country, nor did she have an impressive title. No, she was a wife and a home manager, a woman very much like you and me—just building our homes and holding down the fort (among another thousand and one things!). She also possessed something we should want: a great measure of wisdom.

Meet Abigail. Her story is told in 1 Samuel 25:1-42. She was a woman who had to make a decision every second. Hers was a bitter life. She was married to an alcoholic tyrant named Nabal (meaning "fool"). You can only imagine the tension in their home. Yet Abigail is acclaimed as a woman of wisdom—a woman whose life was characterized by sound and wise conduct, actions, and speech.

Abigail's most amazing act of wisdom was successfully averting a bloodbath between her foolish husband and the avenging warrior David and his 400 men. Abigail knew when to act... and did. She knew what to do...and did it. And she knew what to say...and said it. What were some of the marks of Abigail's wisdom?

She perceived the big picture.
She kept her composure.
She formed a plan.
She spoke with wisdom.
She successfully influenced others.

Abigail's life teaches us that every challenge or responsibility that lies before us can be handled in a better way when we handle it with God's wisdom.

God's Wisdom...for Your Day

Do you desire a better life—one distinguished by greater wisdom and greater success? If this is the desire of your heart, God's Word points to these daily steps.

Step #1—Pray for wisdom. "If any of you lacks wisdom, let him ask of God, who gives to all generously and without reproach, and it will be given to him" (James 1:5). This was what King Solomon did in 2 Chronicles. He recognized his need for wisdom...and acted by asking God for it. Don't major on praying for a good marriage, or obedient children, or money to pay the bills, or a promotion at work. All these desires may be valid and needful, but they are only symptoms of a more valid need—a need for wisdom. Think about it. Wisdom will give you the knowledge and ability to successfully deal with your every need—your everything. Don't merely ask God for help with a symptom. Ask Him for wisdom!

Step #2—Seek wisdom. I love, love, love what Proverbs 2:4-5 says about wisdom: "If you seek her as silver and search for her as for hidden treasures; then you will discern the fear of the LORD and discover the knowledge of God." When I first began studying Proverbs, I remember being impressed by the backbreaking labor and effort it takes a miner to excavate gems, silver, and gold.

Then, while on a ministry trip, Jim and I had an opportunity to go down into a diamond mine. We traveled hundreds of feet below the surface to get to the place where we could observe the gemstones being mined. Like those miners, you and I are going to have to take lots of time to dig daily, energetically, and deeply for wisdom.

Where are we to seek wisdom? The author tells us very plainly, "For the LORD gives wisdom; from His mouth come knowledge and understanding" (Proverbs 2:6). The treasure of the hard-won wisdom needed for a better life comes from the Bible. Do you diligently and strenuously seek the treasure of wisdom? Are you digging through your Bible? Do your personal goals include this assignment from God to seek wisdom? If so, your life will be better day by day as you search the Scriptures and mine its treasures.

Step #3—Grow in wisdom. Solomon is a strong example of a person who desired wisdom, prayed for wisdom, and sought wisdom. Unfortunately, he also provides a negative example of a person who failed in this vital third step: He did not grow in wisdom.

Solomon began well, but allowed himself over the years to be diverted from God and His wisdom. Wisdom is like one of your favorite houseplants. That plant needs water and nutrients to continue to grow. Wisdom, too, needs to be nurtured. Yesterday's wisdom needs to be refreshed, renewed, and expanded today. How is this done? The apostle Peter gives us the answer: "Like newborn babies, long for the pure milk of the word, so that by it you may grow in respect to salvation" (1 Peter 2:2).

9

Creating a Place Called Home
—Homemaking—

Wisdom has built her house,
she has hewn out her seven pillars;
she has prepared her food, she has mixed her wine;
she has also set her table.
PROVERBS 9:1-2

A Prayer to Pray—

Lord, as You empowered Bezalel in the book of Exodus with the wisdom and knowledge needed to create the furnishings for Your Tabernacle, so empower me to create a home that honors You. Help me bless others as I work to create a place where all activities center on You—a place where You are the heart of my home. As You filled the Tabernacle with Your presence, fill me—and my home—with Your Holy Spirit's love, joy, and peace. May my home be a refuge and a little piece of heaven on earth for family and friends. Amen.

If you have read any of my previous books, you know that as I read through my Bible, I like to focus on verses that specifically pertain to women. I can remember very vividly, like it was only yesterday, opening my crisp, new Bible and beginning to read book 1, page 1, chapter 1, verse 1—Genesis 1:1. With my pink marker in hand, I was poised and ready and waiting to make my very first pink mark.[1]

Well, in the time it took me to read 27 verses in Genesis—in the first book of the Bible and the first chapter of the Bible—I hit pay-dirt and made my first ever pink mark in my shiny new Bible. There I discovered the fact that God created "male and female" and charged them to "be fruitful and multiply, and fill the earth, and subdue it" (Genesis 1:27-28). Together the man and woman were to make a home, have a family, and take charge of their surroundings. Obviously, God had a job for the man, but he also gave the woman a job: She was to be his "helper" (Genesis 2:18).

I wondered as I read these opening chapters in my new Bible, What does it mean to be a helper to my husband? With that question burning in my heart, I started on my quest to discover the answer. Over the years, I have studied and written a lot on the idea of being a "helper." One thing that kept coming up in my study was that I can help my husband by providing a place for him and our children to retreat to after a stressful day out in the world.

Whether or not you spend every waking moment within the doors of the place you call home, you can find a way to do whatever it takes to provide a special place for those you love—a little place called home. This is one major way of fulfilling God's design for you to be a helper.

As we come to chapter 9 in the book of Proverbs, I have marked the first six verses in pink. Marking in pink is my way of noting that there is something in these verses that instructs me as a woman, wife, and mother. Here we go!

Wisdom Builds Her Home (Proverbs 9:1-6)

As we step into this new chapter of Proverbs, realize that the author is continuing to define and explain "wisdom." In chapter 8, "Wisdom" was out in the highways and byways, shouting for people to listen to her. Here in chapter 9, she has made a special place in her home for people to come and see firsthand what wisdom has to offer. This place—"her house"—wasn't just something she threw together. No, it was prepared with great effort, time, and care.

Wisdom has built her house (Proverbs 9:1)—The fine lady Wisdom has "built her house, she has hewn out her seven pillars." This shows that she has gone to great lengths to build her house. The "seven pillars" are not explained in detail, but seven is the number of perfection. Perhaps we could say her home was a perfect place for people to come to, a place where their needs would be taken care of. I applied Wisdom's example of building a home in this way:

- Make the effort to build my home. When I say "building," I'm not thinking of a structure or of spending a lot of money. No, a woman's primary focus needs to be on the care that is needed to create a home, not a house. It is built by wisdom, understanding, and knowledge,[2] by ordinary prudence and discretion, and by skillful management and practical and biblical principles.

Wisdom has prepared (Proverbs 9:2)—Wisdom has a plan. Her menu reflects her thoughtfulness, preparation, and the provision of food that nourishes and restores—meat, wine, and all of the appropriate accompanying dishes. Nothing has been left out in her planning.

My personal application?

- Follow in Wisdom's footsteps. You need to pray and work out God's plan for your unique life and the lifestyle God has given you. You have to figure out how you can best help those around you, starting with your family. You probably know this saying: "If you don't plan your day, someone else will be glad to plan it for you!" The more you plan, the greater the potential for success. It is as you pray and plan, and then work out that plan, that your home is built, established, and furnished in a way that honors God and blesses others. When you follow God's plan, your home and its "rooms are filled with all precious and pleasant riches" (Proverbs 24:4).

- Precious and pleasant riches like what? Like love, joy, peace, patience, kindness, goodness, gentleness, faithfulness, and much-needed self-control—the fruit of the Holy Spirit (Galatians 5:22-23). Like an abundance of noble character qualities. Like a patient, loving calmness that ministers to body and soul. Like words that are "sweetness to the soul and health to the bones" (Proverbs 16:24 NKJV). When you follow God's plan, your home will be founded on and furnished with all that is needed for those who dwell within it.

Wisdom has sent out her maidens (Proverbs 9:3-6)—Now that she's ready, Wisdom sends out her servants to spread the news. The simple message is for both the foolish and ignorant—"Forsake your folly," or, as another translation reads, "Leave your foolish ways,"[3] and choose to "proceed in the way of understanding."

- What is the best way to show the world that God's plan for a home and family works? Or the best way to provide a model? Let the world see what all of your building and planning and praying have, by God's grace, produced! Let them see a Spirit-filled marriage. Let them see a family that loves each other and loves Jesus Christ. Let them see the transforming work of God through His Son. Like Wisdom, you can beckon and call out, "Come see for yourselves!" as you put on display a Christ-centered home to a watching world.

Choosing to Build Your Home

Once again, as in previous chapters of Proverbs, God offers His readers an opportunity: "Forsake your folly and live, and proceed in the way of understanding" (Proverbs 9:6). That choice is extended to us: We can choose to follow after wisdom and build our homes, or choose folly and let our homes and home life be inferior, let them crumble and decay with neglect. I believe with all my heart that you care about your home—the people and the place. You want to care—and build. You want what wisdom has to offer. With this as your heart's desire, you will put in the effort. Here are a few practices that will help you stay focused on your home.

Your prayers—Coming before God in prayer lifts the work of homemaking out of the physical realm and transports it into the spiritual realm. Prayer helps you line up your desires with God's plan for you as a woman and homemaker. Praying daily is the vital first step—the starting point—for growing in wisdom...the wisdom that enables you to build a home for your loved ones, a home that blesses all who cross your threshold.

Your purpose—Resolve to be a home builder. Purpose in your heart and in your prayers to live out this role and assignment from God. Then put items on your to-do list that will start and improve the process. Even if creating and caring for a home is not feasible or a burning desire of your heart right now, purpose to follow God's will, no matter what. Then trust Him for the blessings He chooses to pour out and send your way as you follow through as a home builder.

Your presence—Your presence at home is how a home is built, maintained, and enjoyed. You may have a job or responsibilities that take a chunk of your time each day, but when you are home, determine to be all there. Give it your all. Delight in loving your home—the place where those you love reside or visit. A good exercise is to pray as you travel home from your workplace or your out-of-the-home tasks. This will turn your thoughts and energies away from what you've been doing and put your focus fully on what is ahead of you—your home-sweet-home! This practice of prayer will keep you from bringing the problems, issues, emotions, and tiredness from your work and activities into your home.

Anytime you are present at home is time you can love your family and care for your dwelling place. These efforts result in a home built to honor God and serve those who live there. Oh, how blessed they will be...and so will you!

God's Wisdom…for Your Day

In Proverbs 9, God contrasts two kinds of women who are total opposites—"Wisdom" (Proverbs 9:1-6) and "Folly" (verses 13-18). Wisdom is energetic. She actively plans, prepares, prays, and produces a lovely, tranquil home. God paints this picture of Wisdom as a wise woman who is a dedicated homemaker.

But Folly, the opposite of Wisdom, is lazy and doesn't have a clue—or even care—what it means to create a home or to be a helper to her husband or to anyone else. She is "naive and knows nothing." And she sits—yes, "sits at the doorway of her house." And from that doorway, she bellows out to passersby. Just as God describes her, "The woman of folly is boisterous, she is naive and knows nothing."

God's final chilling words about the woman Folly state that others do "not know that the dead are there, that her guests are in the depths of Sheol." As one Bible commentator states,

> Lady Folly's house is not a home but a mausoleum. If you enter it you will not leave it alive.[4]

As a home builder and homemaker for God, you are the giver of life. You are His woman of wisdom who "looks well to the ways of her household, and does not eat the bread of idleness" (Proverbs 31:27). You are the excellent woman who blesses all who cross your path—or your threshold—all who enter your little place called home.

10

Blessing Others with Your Speech —Mouth—

The mouth of the righteous is a fountain of life,
but the mouth of the wicked conceals violence.
PROVERBS 10:11

A Prayer to Pray—

Lord, I can never think of my mouth without recalling these words from the heart of David: "Let the words of my mouth and the meditation of my heart be acceptable in Your sight, O Lord, my rock and my Redeemer." As I contemplate the verse chosen for this chapter, teach me, righteous Father, to think on You so often that my mouth becomes a fountain of goodness and life. Give me the tongue of the learned, that I may be one who speaks a good word in season to those who are weary and in need of encouragement. Amen.

True confession: When I first began reading through one chapter of Proverbs each day, I was frustrated. I just couldn't seem to get a grasp of what the proverbs were trying to tell me. Then one day my mentor suggested I start coding the proverbs, looking for and coding common themes as I read. Well, what woman doesn't have a problem with her mouth? So I chose the letter "M" for "mouth," and amazingly, with one glance I can see that 11 out of the 32 verses in Proverbs, chapter 10, address the subject of the mouth, our speech, and in my case, also my teaching.

As I tackled the subject of the mouth, tongue, speech, and communication, conviction and instruction came to me like a tsunami. This key subject in Proverbs called for much time spent researching and trying to apply the wisdom from Proverbs in my daily life, my marriage relationship, with my children, and even as I ministered to women at church.

And just a note: As we begin this section (Proverbs, chapters 10–24) you will note some changes. These are "the proverbs of Solomon" (Proverbs 10:1). In this new section, we will be looking at a random assortment of proverbs. Most of the 15 chapters in this section will address selected proverbs that, when taken to heart, provide opportunities for us to choose to correct our bad attitudes and actions—what we think and say.

Blessing Begins with Righteous Living

We first encountered the word "righteousness" in Proverbs 1:3 where it is connected with wisdom—"to receive instruction in wise behavior, righteousness, justice and equity." After this initial statement, "righteous" or "righteousness" is repeated over 90 times in the book of Proverbs. Throughout Proverbs, the righteous are seen as walking straight paths of integrity and uprightness. Their plans and actions are just. They are generous, careful, and keep God's law and obey His commands. These are the actions of the righteous. Simply stated, they are good people who do good things.

It's sad but true that the actions of the wicked are just the opposite. This contrast spills over to include the speech of the righteous as compared to that of the wicked—speech that is harsh, harmful, and violent.

As a child of God, you're probably much more interested in the speech of those who are righteous. I know I am! So for our purposes, what do the words of the righteous produce?

The words of the righteous offer life—"The mouth of the righteous is a fountain of life, but the mouth of the wicked conceals violence" (Proverbs 10:11). Those living at the time of Solomon would know exactly the picture that was being painted with these words. Water, both then and now, is the most precious commodity in the deserts of the Middle East. And believe me, I know because I have experienced these arid conditions myself! I can still vividly remember my first visit to the Middle East. Forget food! All we focused on was making sure we took a precious bottle of water along with us. What we craved was water!

The temperature was at least 110 degrees outside as we trekked mile after mile through the Sahara. Jim and I were on a very unique tour that was scheduled to take us from our present location, Egypt, to the countries of Lebanon, Syria, Jordan, and then into Israel. It was an adventure I will never forget. You learn on Day 1 to value a drink of water more than food!

But at that moment we were on our way to visit a Bedouin settlement in the middle of the desert. As we neared our destination, I noticed a large number of palm trees. The area was lush with lots of green plants and a large pool of water and camels! The camp was settled around an oasis, with water welling up from the ground. That water flowing into the oasis provided life for everything and everyone who came into contact with it. Without that fountain, there would be only death!

That oasis fountain is a picture of the life-giving refreshment that you can offer as you speak to others. A fountain can do nothing but spring up, make a joyful sound, and issue forth life-giving water from the earth. Its waters flow on and on. When you seek righteousness and to be righteous, wherever you are and whomever you speak with, your mouth will overflow with words of kindness and encouragement. You will be the bringer of refreshment—and life.

The words of the righteous offer value—"The tongue of the righteous is as choice silver, the heart of the wicked is worth little" (Proverbs 10:20). Recently, when Jim and I were in Mexico for ministry, our event organizer took us on a tour of the Aztec pyramids outside Mexico City. Afterward we visited a local silversmith, where we were able to watch every step involved in producing choice silver and the craftsmanship that resulted in many exquisite, hand-tooled silver rings, bracelets, and necklaces. They were amazing…because they were "choice silver." Well, thinking ahead to my upcoming birthday, my sweet Jim purchased me a little choker necklace.

Whenever I wear this precious-to-me necklace from my husband, I think of this proverb. Like my necklace of choice silver, a good woman's words are of value. They are not just idle chatter. When she opens her mouth, people lean forward in anticipation of what wonderful, genuine, choice words of wisdom and refreshment she is going to share. Unlike her sterling words, those uttered out of "the heart of the wicked is worth little." The good woman's words, which come from a pure sterling heart, are of great value, while the words from a wicked heart are valueless.

The words of the righteous offer help—"The lips of the righteous feed many" (Proverbs 10:21). In my Bible, this verse has an "M" for mouth beside it—and also a "T" notation. That's because when I read this verse I also picture in my mind the "teaching" ("T") of God's Word. A righteous teacher, male or female, not only feeds themselves as they study, but out of that study they also give spiritual food to those who listen. As a Bible teacher and author, I repeatedly read—and pray—this verse. My desire is to give spiritual help and encouragement as I am privileged to write and speak to women.

By contrast, "fools die for lack of understanding." This proverb could be paraphrased, "Good feeds itself and others, but evil cannot even keep itself alive."[1]

The words of the righteous offer wisdom—"The mouth of the righteous flows with wisdom, but the perverted tongue will be cut out" (Proverbs 10:31). In my book *Beautiful in God's Eyes,*[2] I describe another trip I was privileged to take with my husband as he accompanied a group of seminary students on a three-week study tour in Israel. On one of our daily tours, we were bused to the Dead Sea, which gets its name for a good reason. The fresh water of the Jordan River flows into this sea—but nothing flows out. The water is highly saline, therefore nothing lives in its waters. It is literally a "dead" sea.

Later that same day, we traveled to a place called Ein Gedi (translated "spring of the goat"), where we experienced the opposite of the Dead Sea. There was a magnificent waterfall, a deep blue pool, and a crystal clear stream flowing down a natural, elevated stone walkway. It was such a refreshing blessing and relief from the scorching dry heat that most of the students swam or waded in that cool, refreshing spring.

In my head and heart, this spring is my picture of the righteous woman's words. Her words not only provide life and help, but also refreshing wisdom. I've known quite a few of these wise, vibrant women over the years, and I've tried to spend as much time as possible with them. I wanted what they had to offer—wisdom, joy, encouragement, and excitement. I hope you noted the contrast between the tongue of the righteous and that of the perverted. A good person's words will be like a tree that brings forth blossoms of wisdom. But the person whose words are crooked or perverted will be like a tree that has no purpose and is cut down.

The words of the righteous are worthy—"The lips of the righteous bring forth what is acceptable" (Proverbs 10:32). As part of my journey to Christ, I began to seek "something" week after week as I visited church after church and a multitude of odd religious gatherings. Consciously, I couldn't have told you what I was seeking. But every time I left one of those religious gatherings, I knew in my heart something about their message wasn't right. That lack of acceptance kept me looking, and looking, and looking…

…until Jesus Christ found me. He found me right in my own home as I was reading the only Bible in our house—one given to me as a child. What that book—the Bible—was saying was acceptable to my heart. It made sense. It had answers—real answers—to my questions. What it was saying was worthy of my time and consideration. Its message filled a void in my heart and soul. And it led me to accept the fact that Jesus Christ was God, and I could follow Him!

And now, here in Proverbs 10:32, God is telling us this is

exactly the kind of speech He wants us to share. He wants us to bless others with our speech—to speak what is true, helpful, edifying, good, wholesome, worthy, acceptable, and full of grace.

Since embracing Christ as my Savior and enjoying many years of spiritual growth, I have tried to be this kind of person and teacher—one whose lips bring forth what is acceptable. This, my reading friend, is what God wants for His women—for you and for me! May we put far away what is perverse and wicked, and speak only what is worthy of the Lord and of us as women who belong to the Lord.

God's Wisdom...for Your Day

We are so blessed that the book of Proverbs is tucked right in the middle of the Bible! It makes it super easy to find! In this book, God presents words of wisdom that tell His people how to live and walk and talk with wisdom. As you approach your day, put these few words of wisdom to work in your speech and interactions with those who will cross your path today:

Think before you speak—"On the lips of the discerning, wisdom is found, but a rod is for the back of him who lacks understanding" (Proverbs 10:13). Make it your goal to carefully select words and wording that measure up to God's standards of wisdom and kindness.

Wait before you speak—"Wise men store up knowledge, but with the mouth of the foolish, ruin is at hand" (Proverbs 10:14). You may have heard the saying, "It's better to be thought a fool, than to open your mouth and prove it." Unfortunately, this is all too true! Waiting, rather than blurting something out, will allow you to hear all the facts, weigh the facts, consider who you are talking to, and most important, allow you to calm down—and offer a quick prayer before you speak!

Err on the side of less when you speak—"When there are many words, transgression is unavoidable, but he who restrains his lips is wise" (Proverbs 10:19). I'm sure you've experienced the sinking feeling you get when you keep talking and explaining and filling every space of silence with nervous talk. It's almost like the more you say and the longer your jabbering continues, the deeper the hole you dig. This problem is easily solved: Think to yourself, "Less is best!" [And P.S.—that's the message Jesus conveyed in these few words: "Let your 'Yes' be 'Yes,' and your 'No,' 'No' " (Matthew 5:37 NKJV).]

My prayer for you and myself is that we bless others with our speech. May we be like God's excellent woman who "opens her mouth in wisdom, and the teaching of kindness is on her tongue" (Proverbs 31:26). Like her, may our hearts be righteous. And may the words of our mouths that spring forth from our hearts improve, better, and bless the lives of those who hear.

11

Enriching Your Character —Virtues—

He who is steadfast in righteousness will attain to life, and he who pursues evil will bring about his own death.

PROVERBS 11:19

A Prayer to Pray—

Dear God in heaven, my greatest desire is that, like a tree planted near rivers of water whose leaf does not wither, I too would daily plant my heart near You. I want to exhibit righteous behavior and godly virtues that will be a sign to those I encounter today of Your Son's life in me, and a beacon of light drawing others to my matchless Savior. Amen.

You probably have your own personal favorite verses in the Bible that you read over and over, maybe have even memorized. They are so rich and desirable that they can become your "theme verses" for certain aspects of your life. One verse my husband, Jim, and I claimed as our theme verse for marriage is Luke 1:6. It gives a striking description of Zacharias and Elizabeth, who would later become the parents of John the Baptist:

> *They were both righteous in the sight of God,*
> *walking blamelessly in all the commandments*
> *and requirements of the LORD.*

The amazing thing about this couple and their life together is that they had never known the much-cherished and desired blessing of having children. For parents in ancient times to be childless was generally seen as a curse from God. Yet this "righteous" couple did not turn their backs on God or give half-hearted, lukewarm assent to God. In spite of their personal problems and pained hearts, they trusted and followed God's commands completely and wholeheartedly.

In the previous chapter in this book, we learned what it means to be "righteous" and the effects of the speech of a "righteous" person. In the Old Testament—and especially in the book of Proverbs—a righteous person was a good person who did good things, who therefore was a blessing to others. In the New Testament, the same results occurred in the lives of Zacharias and Elizabeth. Because they were obedient to the commands of Scripture—the "requirements of the Lord"—in their old age, God blessed them and the world by giving them a child, John the Baptist, the forerunner of the Lord Jesus Christ! Not only were Zacharias and Elizabeth blessed with a child, but their child grew up to bless a multitude of others. As the herald, John the

Baptist pointed the people to the coming of the Messiah and prepared them for "the salvation of God" through repentance.

Nurturing Godly Character Qualities

Here in chapter 11 of Proverbs, we continue to see a random collection of wise sayings from the pen of King Solomon. In them we learn what happens when a good or righteous person strives for positive behavior and seeks God's help in eliminating negative, sinful, unrighteous behavior. God has much to teach us about the importance of paying close attention to nurturing and honing godly character qualities!

Honesty versus dishonesty—If you look up the dictionary definition for "integrity," you'll discover it means being truthful, trustworthy, and having convictions, all of which means such a person is "upright." A man or woman who has integrity is an honest person. You can count on them to do the right thing for the right reason, even when no one is watching. They have character and are guided by a set of biblical and moral principles that keep them on God's straight and narrow path.

By contrast, the dishonest or treacherous person has few or no convictions or moral standards. This crooked person therefore follows the path of least resistance, which is indeed crooked. The writer of Proverbs tells us what rewards are received by each of these two kinds of people:

> *The integrity of the upright will guide them,*
> *but the crookedness of the treacherous will destroy them.*
> (Proverbs 11:3)

The dishonest, treacherous, crooked person with no morals will be destroyed by his own evil. Because of their evil, they miss out on "real life," on the daily joys and blessings righteous living brings. Even more tragically, they miss out on heaven! How unfortunate that a person would choose a present life of dishonesty rather than a future life without tears, sorrow, pain, and sin rather than a place of eternal life basking in the presence and glory of Almighty God and His eternal Son, our Savior, the Lord Jesus Christ!

The person of integrity and virtue will be guided to what is right and can live—really live!—and enjoy life to its fullest. And there is no fear of the future, for God's gift of eternal life awaits them.

I love these words from an unknown source: "A person is not given integrity. It results from the relentless pursuit of honesty at all times." Lord, make us relentless in our pursuit of honesty!

Gossip versus silence—You've probably heard or seen the term "talebearer" at some time in your life. While researching exactly what this word means, I found this lively definition: A talebearer is a blabbermouth! I'm sure you know exactly what this means. And I'm sure you know certain individuals in your workplace, neighborhood, and maybe even at church who salivate over what they hear or see and instantly begin to blab and spread the word!

Talebearers can't be trusted to use wisdom and self-discipline to keep quiet about what they hear—which may not even be true. They simply lack the virtues of wisdom and discretion. And worse than these shortcomings is the fact that they lack love. They don't love the person they are talking about, for "love covers a multitude of sins."[1]

In my book *A Woman After God's Own Heart*,[2] I wrote extensively about my own problem with gossip as a new believer. Recognizing and admitting my problem, I began to pay attention to what the Bible says about a person who gossips. To my shock, I discovered the book of Proverbs paints a sad and alarming picture of the destruction and damage that come from a person who gossips. For instance...

- A gossip betrays a confidence (Proverbs 11:13; 20:19). "He who goes about as a talebearer reveals secrets, but he who is trustworthy conceals a matter," and "He who goes about as a slanderer reveals secrets, therefore do not associate with a gossip."

- A gossip separates close friends (Proverbs 16:28). "A perverse man spreads strife, and a slanderer separates intimate friends."

- A gossip keeps things stirred up (Proverbs 26:20). "For lack of wood the fire goes out, and where there is no whisperer, contention quiets down."

The more I studied and searched the Scriptures, the more sick I became—sick of myself and sick of my sin. What was the remedy for ridding gossip from my life? First, I called what I was doing exactly what it is—gossip is sin. Then I asked God to work mightily in my life, my heart—and my mouth! Based on Proverbs 11:13 ("He who is trustworthy conceals a matter"), I chose to know nothing. I didn't want to know anything about anybody. And if by accident I heard something, I chose to say nothing, to keep silent. I can only thank and praise God that this hard lesson was learned and corrected in my first few years as a Christian!

As you read daily through the book of Proverbs, you will learn that the proverbs are an extremely practical source for instruction on how to live a righteous and godly life—a life of character—and that includes a life without gossip!

Grace and discretion—The greatest honor a woman can receive is the praise and admiration from those closest to her. As we walk with the Lord and follow His Word, our life will be a portrait of grace and virtue. It will be just as God says:

> *A gracious woman attains honor.*
> (Proverbs 11:16)

Without seeking honor, recognition, popularity, or attention, we will attain honor and respect, and receive praise from others, starting with those at home. Our family will be blessed. So will our husband and children. Our close friends and acquaintances at work, next door, and in a Bible study at church will respond to our gracious ways. It's a given: As God states, a gracious woman attains honor.

Unlike the world we live in, God is not interested in our outward beauty. In fact, He paints this ludicrous picture of "beauty":

> *As a ring of gold in a swine's snout*
> *so is a beautiful woman who lacks discretion.*
> (Proverbs 11:22)

Just imagine a pig with a gold nose ring on its snout, which is used to root through garbage, mud, and debris! Why put such a beautiful ornament on such an unworthy body? It's ridiculous, right? This is the comparison to a beautiful woman who shows no discretion, no maturity, no tact, no wisdom. She may have external beauty, but that's all she has, and by her actions, she acts like a lowly beast that wallows in the mud and mire.

No, God fixes His premium on inner beauty—on our

excellent virtues. On our godly qualities. On our Christlike virtues like righteousness, graciousness, and much-needed discretion. God especially approves of a woman who "fears the Lord," as these proverbs state:

> *Charm is deceitful and beauty is vain,*
> *but a woman who fears the* Lord*,*
> *she shall be praised.*
> (Proverbs 31:30)

God's Wisdom...for Your Day

I've already shared that as a new Christian coming out of the world, every time I found a passage that spoke to me as a woman, I marked it with my pink marker. And today, as I continue to read through my Bible, these "pink passages" that specifically mention something about women continue to remind me how I am supposed to talk and act as a woman of God.

Whether you mark your Bible or not, keep reading it each and every day. This daily practice is how you will enrich your character and strengthen godly virtues. This daily discipline is where graciousness is defined and discretion is grown. This daily habit is where honesty is honed and gossip is hushed and banished.

And keep reading the book of Proverbs, one chapter each day. You are a different person today than you were yesterday. Yesterday is gone. Each "today" arrives with a whole new set of problems—or maybe with the challenge of continuing to handle the old, ongoing ones! And, as you well know, each day has its possible roadblocks, detours, speed bumps, and catastrophes.

Hopefully, you are gaining wisdom and instruction from the Bible for yesterday's problems. But I repeat, today is a new day—*your* new day. It's also the day the Lord has given to you, with a whole set of new challenges and responsibilities God wants to help you handle. Let Him guide your steps through your day. Open your Bible and open your heart and pray, "Open my eyes, that I may behold wonderful things from Your law" (Psalm 119:18).

Be encouraged, my friend. In His Word, God gives you everything you need to handle anything that comes your way and in your day in a godly way—His way. You can start every day of your life with these divine words of truth and promise:

> *Grace and peace be multiplied to you in the knowledge of God and of Jesus our Lord; seeing that His divine power has granted to us everything pertaining to life and godliness, through the true knowledge of Him who has called us by His own glory and excellence. For by these He has granted to us His precious and magnificent promises, so that by them you may become partakers of the divine nature* (2 Peter 1:2-4).

12

Growing Smarter Each Day —Teachable—

The way of a fool is right in his own eyes,
but a wise man is he who listens to counsel.
PROVERBS 12:15

A Prayer to Pray—

O fountain of all that is good, I come before You this fresh, new day with a heart that can so easily be stubborn and rebellious. Too often in my pride and foolishness I choose to make my own way and trust in my own limited wisdom, resisting Your perfect counsel and Your wise input through Your Word. Today I submit to Your wisdom. Please, Father, teach me and lead me in Your everlasting ways. Amen.

You probably know this saying: "Confession is good for the soul, but bad for the reputation." Well, here goes! When we became a Christian family, Jim and I were desperate to turn things around in all areas of our lives, and the sooner the better! Obviously, our first step was to get plugged into a Bible teaching church. Then, as we began to read and study the Bible, we realized that the Bible had answers to our every need, problem, question, and issue—*all* the answers!

You can't imagine our complete joy when, *Eureka!* we discovered that the book of Proverbs was a gold mine of wisdom. We wanted to grow quickly, and Proverbs gave us answers to our questions, "How can we be smarter and wiser today than we were yesterday? How can we grow today?"

The True Path to Wisdom Is a Teachable Spirit

Here is a handful of proverbs that guide us toward wisdom. Every single one of them tells us to listen to counsel, to surround ourselves with an abundance of counselors, to pay attention to reproof and correction, and to purposefully increase in wisdom. Put simply, the true path to wisdom is a teachable spirit.

Learn from the experiences of others—"The way of a fool is right in his own eyes, but a wise man is he who listens to counsel" (Proverbs 12:15). Here's a principle I heard in a teacher training seminar: "He who depends upon his own experiences has relatively little material to work with." Well, coming out of the world, I had plenty of experience, but it was mostly the wrong kind. As I said, I desperately needed help, especially with strengthening my marriage and raising two little toddlers. So, in addition to reading my Bible, I took the advice of multiple proverbs like this one (12:15) and started looking for others who could help me in my growth as a Christian woman.

I looked around my new church and observed the women who seemed to have their act together in the areas of marriage, parenting, ministry, and personal growth and discipline. It didn't matter if the woman was younger than me. If she exhibited a quality the Bible said I needed, I asked that woman for help, instruction, and advice.

Proverbs 12:15 contrasts two kinds of people. The first is a fool: "The way of a fool is right in his own eyes." This foolish person is not seeking help or wisdom from others. Instead, he mistakenly thinks he already knows everything. But the second person is wise: "A wise man is he who listens to counsel." Seeking—and listening—to counsel is a mark of a woman who is wise.

This shouldn't be a foreign concept. Think about the many people who hire consultants, coaches, trainers, nutritionists, and efficiency experts to help them improve their personal life or their business. But you? You don't have to hire a single person! God has given you the full counsel of the Lord in His Word. And He has also given you other Christians who are mature, experienced, and can give you wise counsel.

And guess what? My first, greatest blessing was realizing that they were waiting—yes, waiting—to be a "Titus 2" woman for women like me who were new in the faith and needed help understanding God's plan for our lives.[1]

You too can look around your church for Titus 2 women. These ladies are available to guide and instruct you through difficult times and the seasons of life. These more mature women are God's army of angelic experts, ready to help you grow your spiritual wings. The Bible teaches that "older women…are to be…teaching what is good, so that they may encourage the young women…" (see Titus 2:3-5). Their responsibility is to set an example and teach and encourage you. Your responsibility is to seek them out, ask your questions, and be a wise woman "who listens to counsel."

Seek multiple opinions—"Where there is no guidance the people fall, but in abundance of counselors there is victory" (Proverbs 11:14). This proverb originally contrasted a nation that falls because of a lack of counsel with a nation that enjoys victory because of their many seasoned advisers. This is also true for you and me. When you must make important decisions regarding your health, finances, marriage, family, job, your children's education, and more, be sure you gather opinions and advice from several people you respect—people who are wise and experienced.

The wisdom contained in Proverbs 11:14 is your safeguard. If you rely on yourself, your feelings, your limited knowledge, and your best friends or coworkers (who may tell you what you *want* to hear), you may make a decision that takes you in the wrong direction. By seeking multiple opinions, you are gathering the collective wisdom, knowledge, and experience of others. Sit at their feet. Soak up their advice. God promises the independent, ignorant, self-sufficient, proud fool will fall. And, praise Him, He promises the humble seeker of God's will and truth will experience victory.

Accept the reproof of others—"Do not reprove a scoffer, or he will hate you, reprove a wise man and he will love you" (Proverbs 9:8). How do you usually handle criticism? And what's your attitude or response when someone gives you advice you didn't ask for—or don't like? This is a test that reveals whether you are in the "scoffer" category or the "wise" woman category. Which are you? "Wise people receive reproof and rebuke with appreciation; fools do not."[2]

Writing to his two teenage sons, an author and father explained Proverbs 9:8 with these straightforward, easy-to-understand words and advice:

> The way in which a man receives rebuke is an index of his character. A scoffer hates you, whereas a wise man will thank you...Instead of resenting criticism, a wise man takes it to heart and thus becomes wiser.[3]

Be a lifelong learner—"Give instruction to a wise man and he will be still wiser, teach a righteous man and he will increase his learning" (Proverbs 9:9). This proverb speaks of the ongoing process of imparting—and receiving—wisdom. I love God's account of Jesus' progression to adulthood in Luke 2:52:

> *And Jesus kept increasing in wisdom and stature, and in favor with God and men.*

Jesus followed the normal path toward maturity. His life was one of progression, and that should be our goal as well—to grow wiser and smarter each day, as well as more spiritually mature. Each day God allows us to live is a day to learn something new and different. How can you insure that each day moves you forward in learning and growing?

Read!—A key way to grow from the experiences of others is by reading the books written by believers and godly women. For instance, do you have a problem in some issue or role in your life? If so, find a Christian author who has answers for you in this area. Read how he or she dealt with that same problem. Learn from the scriptures the writer shares. Grow in wisdom as you apply wise principles to your problem. That author has spent years struggling and researching and dealing with your same issue, and now he or she is offering you biblical help to gain victory in that area. Just think: Possibly ten years or more of their experience is contained in a single book, and it's yours for only a few dollars and a few hours of reading time. What a deal!

Ask questions—Not just any questions, but the right questions—questions that will expand your understanding of the Bible and how it applies to your life and your problems. Remember that you are a learner. This means every person can teach you something. They may even be an expert in some area. Find out what that something is, and then learn from them.

You've heard it before: There's no such thing as a dumb question. So don't be afraid to ask questions. A question never asked is information never learned. Ask questions...and you just might learn something of great benefit to you, something life-changing!

Stretch yourself—"Whoever loves discipline loves knowledge, but he who hates reproof is stupid" (Proverbs 12:1). The word "discipline" can also be translated "instruction." The idea is that learning, knowledge, or wisdom doesn't come easily. All these pursuits require effort. So the effort of discipline as described in Proverbs 12:1 is how you continue being a lifelong learner.

There may come a time in your life when you become comfortable with your level of knowledge and your roles and responsibilities. Things are going well at home, and you are performing okay on your job and in your ministry while taking care of your day-to-day activities and commitments. Everything is easy-peasy. Your personal or ministry challenges have leveled out, and you feel like you know what you're doing.

This happened to me. For two decades I had sought spiritual

growth, nurtured my marriage, was a hands-on mom, and accepted any ministry challenge that came my way at church. Then one day I woke up, and all was well...and quiet. Both of my daughters were married. And there I was, doing the same things over and over, wondering, "Is this it? Have I arrived? Lord, what's next?"

It was then through God's leading that I chose to take up a new and totally different—and mega-challenging—pursuit: I wrote a book! It was almost like as soon as I began to talk earnestly to God about my "status quo" condition...suddenly, out of the blue, a publisher called me (!) and wanted to know if I would consider writing a book.

Talk about growth! Talk about learning something (no, make that many somethings) new! Talk about stretching yourself! And talk about discipline! Whew...that was about 100 books ago, as I grew in a completely foreign area. And each of these 100 books and Bible studies has brought with it the need for me to do more Bible research (growth), work on improving my writing skills (instruction), and create a completely new way of managing my time (direction).

Don't be like the Dead Sea. Don't stagnate! S-t-r-e-t-c-h yourself! Each day ask:

> "What new thing can I learn today?"
> "Who can I learn from today?"
> "How can I be stretched in some aspect of my life today?"

Be willing to pay the price—When Jesus spoke of heaven, He likened it to a merchant seeking fine pearls. When the merchant found "one pearl of great value, he went and sold all that he had and bought it."[4] When you want to learn and grow in wisdom and in your Christian life, it will come at a cost. It takes time to read and study the Bible—and the proverbs. It takes time to meet with another woman for direction, accountability, and counsel. It takes time—and money—to read books that are filled with wisdom and instruction, to work your way through a personal Bible study, to attend a conference taught by gifted speakers.

Yes, increasing in wisdom takes time—and sometimes money—but the reward is great. It will please God and bless others as you share the wisdom you have sought—and gained!

God's Wisdom...for Your Day

I thank God that one of my early mentors suggested I pick five topics I was interested in and passionate about to research and study. Well, I took this assignment to heart and began my study, and today much of what I learned over the years in the five areas I selected, you are now reading in my books. So this is my same challenge to you. Today pick out five areas of interest and start the learning process—or at least begin praying about what those topics might be. Who knows? Maybe in a few years, I'll be reading your books!

...Which leads me to this one last word of encouragement: What you are learning is not just for yourself. God wants you to learn and grow...and pass that knowledge and experience on to others. That's God plan for you—that you pass on what you know and have learned, that you be "teaching what is good...encourag[ing] the young women" (Titus 2:3-4).

As you follow God's wise advice to you to be a woman who is faithful to ask others for counsel and advice, ask Him to lead you to the right people. Here's a prayer you can use today and anytime you are looking for godly guidance:

> *Lord, I ask You to show me how I should seek advice. Reveal to me the people who can give me wise advice. Teach me how to discern and use the counsel I receive. Help me to grow and learn so that I can give good counsel to others who have need.*[5]

13

Speaking the Truth —Words—

From the fruit of a man's mouth he enjoys good,
but the desire of the treacherous is violence.
The one who guards his mouth preserves his life;
the one who opens wide his lips comes to ruin.

PROVERBS 13:2-3

A Prayer to Pray—

O Omnipresent Lord, today I come before Your throne of holiness asking for help with my tongue. It shames me to know that every careless, thoughtless, and hurtful word I've spoken has been heard and noted by You. But praise be for Your Holy Son, that in Jesus I have forgiveness. I purpose today to set a guard over my mouth, that no unwholesome word would proceed out of my mouth. May my speech be praise for You and that which is true, edifying, and encouraging to others. Amen.

The mouth and a person's speech is a v-e-r-y common theme in Proverbs! You would expect that from a book in the Bible that targets and exalts wisdom, wouldn't you? Maybe that's because speech is such a monumental, disgusting, minute-by-minute daily problem!

Chapter 13 of Proverbs opens with verses 2 and 3—two verses that deal with a person's mouth. Many other scriptures about our speech are sprinkled throughout Proverbs and are a constant reminder of how we are to talk, and what we are to say and not say when we do talk. By now you know that the book of Proverbs is extremely practical. It addresses just about every problem you will ever have, right down to the very words that come out of your mouth! Like the book of Proverbs, this simple children's Sunday school chorus has a powerful message:

> Be careful little lips what you say,
> for the Father up above
> is looking down with love,
> so be careful little lips what you say.

Our speech is a key element—and challenge—in our daily life. Our words reveal what we are and what we are thinking. If our words are this important, then greater knowledge of the proverbs that address this key mark of wisdom can only help us. In Proverbs, God gives us His instructions for handling this major problem area of the tongue. He even tells us the kind of words we should choose to use and not use, and gives us a generous amount of advice for this daily challenge. You and I have help and hope because instructions in Proverbs show us how to gain victory over our mouth.

As you make your way through the proverbs in this chapter and additional proverbs that address the mouth and speech, you will observe the positive effects of right speech. You will also see that the wrong kinds of speech produce bad or negative results. Always remember, your words have great weight. They will always produce an effect—either for good or for evil.

Three Truths About Words

The effects of right speech—"From the fruit of a man's mouth he enjoys good, but the desire of the treacherous is violence" (Proverbs 13:2). The vast majority of references to "fruit" in the Bible depict it as the result of some activity. Here in this proverb we see that a person's reasonable speech will produce good results, good fruit. This same idea is seen in two other proverbs: "A man will be satisfied with good by the fruit of his words" (12:14) and "With the fruit of a man's mouth his stomach will be satisfied; he will be satisfied with the product of his lips" (18:20). Now that you know more about the positive effects of right speech, how can you be more sensitive to your word choices? Proverbs 10:11 gives us the answer: "The mouth of the righteous is a fountain of life." Obviously, a righteous heart and life will yield right speech. To be a woman who utters what is right, make sure your heart is right.

The consequences of unguarded speech—"The one who guards his mouth preserves his life; the one who opens wide his lips comes to ruin" (Proverbs 13:3). What we say can get us into much more trouble than what we do. For instance, think about the last time you ended up buying something at too high a price because you said yes too soon. Or consider the credibility you lost because you let something slip and betrayed a confidence.

Clearly, the one who lacks self-control when it comes to his or her mouth is in big trouble. The lesson from this proverb is,

Be careful what you say…it just might be your downfall, your ruin. Or, as Benjamin Franklin put it, "Better slip with foot than tongue."[1]

The book of James in the New Testament has been referred to as "a book of wisdom." Here are some facts about the tongue that should serve as a wake-up call for all women to guard their speech. James describes the nature of the tongue in James 3:6. The tongue is:

> a fire,
> the very world of iniquity,
> can defile the body,
> sets on fire the course of your life, and
> is set on fire by hell.

In the words of John Calvin, "This slender portion of flesh contains the whole world of iniquity."

Unfortunately, we are masters of making excuses for the unrestrained use of the tongue. We say:

> "Somebody had to tell him off."
> "It was good to get it off my chest."
> "I sure gave her a piece of my mind."
> "Maybe what I said will do him some good."
> "I feel better for saying it."[2]

There is something we can do about our speech. "Instead of making excuses for sounding off, we can exercise restraint and allow God's peace and wisdom to guide what we say."[3]

The benefits of truthful speech—"Truthful lips will be established forever, but a lying tongue is only for a moment" (Proverbs 12:19). Truth is an amazing and wonderful thing: You never have to remember what you said if you always tell the truth. And yet everyone is tempted to lie, even though lying is so evil and so bad that it is counted as one of the "seven things" on God's list of things He hates. In fact, God considers lying "an abomination to Him."[4] Realizing the serious nature of lying should give every woman second and even third thoughts about speaking the truth versus lying, even about telling "half-truths," which, as you already know, are in reality lies.

Three Words to the Wise

Talking too much leads to sin—"When there are many words, transgression is unavoidable, but he who restrains his lips is wise" (Proverbs 10:19). It stands to reason that the more you talk, the greater the probability of saying something wrong, mean, evil, or ugly. Another translation states, "In the multitude of words sin is not lacking" (NKJV). Compulsive talking ultimately leads to exaggerations, the breaking of confidences, and the making of foolish statements—most of which are labeled as sinful behavior in the Bible.

This makes the opposite speech pattern the mark of wisdom: "He who restrains his lips is wise" (Proverbs 10:19). Or, as another translation says, "Where there is much talk there will be no end to sin; but he who keeps his mouth shut does wisely."[5] When you exercise self-control in your speech, you are being—and being seen as—a wise woman. You also save yourself from embarrassment, apologies, and the need to ask forgiveness from God and those your words have harmed or destroyed. When it comes to speech, never forget that "words are so powerful that silence is sometimes the wisest action."[6] Be safe instead of sorry. Make this your motto and guide to wisdom: Less is best!

Words can kill or heal—"There is one who speaks rashly like the thrusts of a sword, but the tongue of the wise brings healing" (Proverbs 12:18). Clearly our words can be used to hurt others or heal others. We already know this from personal experience—from having hurt someone with our harsh words, angry words, destructive words, or slanderous words. Unfortunately, I heard a tragic story of a mother who shared at the funeral of her son who had committed suicide that false rumors about her son were what drove him to take his own life.

Thank the Lord that we are also able to deliver words that heal—soft words, comforting words, encouraging words, words of love, words of appreciation, words of counsel, and words of prayer.

Cruel words can cut—and obviously kill—as deeply as the thrust of a sword or the scorch of a fire. James echoed this same truth when he wrote, "The tongue is set among our members as that which defiles the entire body, and sets on fire the course of our life, and is set on fire by hell" (James 3:6). I bookmarked this anonymous poem while researching this topic in Proverbs, entitled "Sins of the Tongue":

> Only a word of anger
> But it wounded one sensitive heart;
> Only a word of sharp reproach,
> But it made the teardrops start;
> Only a hasty, thoughtless word,
> Sarcastic and unkind;
> But it darkened the day before so bright
> And left a sting behind.[7]

I'm sure you can relate to the heart cries behind these words—I know I cried when I first read this. There are definite lessons to learn from this poetry! But again, aren't you glad that the tongue also has the opportunity to bring health and healing? As two other proverbs instruct us, "A soothing tongue is a tree of life" (15:4) and "A gentle answer turns away wrath" (15:1). I came across these words that can serve as a checklist for your speech:

> Watch your comments about situations. Are you consistently negative? Or do you look for and speak about the positive? Monitor your speech and deliberately choose positive words. A positive attitude creates more positives. Ask God to help you keep a guard on your tongue. He will teach you how to speak words of honest wisdom and loving-kindness.[8]

You and I always have a choice when we open our mouths: We can choose words that harm—or words that heal. Remember: You have not mastered self-control if you have not mastered what you say and don't say.

As I was writing the paragraph above, I couldn't stop thinking about chocolate! More specifically, about a box full of chocolates. If you're like me (and are lucky enough to have a box of chocolates!), you peer into that box of delicious delicacies and oh-so-slowly, oh-so-carefully select which one you will eat. We already know that every single one of them is sweet and delicious, a real treat! And very carefully we take the time to pick out one, just one—the one—that will be the most satisfying.

As women after God's own heart, let's determine first of all that we will seek to deliver only words that are "chocolate" to another person—words that are good, sweet, special, a pick-me-up. Words that are comforting and wise that will minister to the person and to their individual need. As you talk with the women who cross your path, listen to their hearts as they share. Discern their needs. Then consider all of the good things you could say, and choose the perfect one to bless them.

Wisdom imparts knowledge when it speaks—"The tongue of the wise makes knowledge acceptable, but the mouth of fools spouts folly" (Proverbs 15:2). Other proverbs describe the fool who speaks, even when he has nothing to say (see Proverbs 12:23 and 13:16). The wise woman, on the other hand, may speak less frequently, but when she does speak, she has something worthwhile to say. Her tongue speaks words that are acceptable and appropriate—and bear the mark of wisdom.

Many women have a hard time keeping their mouth shut. For some reason, we feel compelled to offer an opinion or give a personal bit of advice on almost every subject…or to make sure we have the last word! We know women—and have been "that woman"—with a "smart mouth" who is the jabber mouth, the know-it-all person, the entertainer, the last-word woman. So what is God's solution to our tendency to run off at the mouth?

As the majority of the proverbs that speak of the mouth say, we should resist these temptations and choose to listen…rather than talk. Why not choose to listen to others? Don't miss out on the potential contribution listening to others makes in us, which in turn makes us wiser. That's the message of Proverbs 9:9: "Give instruction to a wise man and he will be still wiser."

God's Wisdom...for Your Day

Would you change the way you live if you knew that your every word and thought would be examined by God? David asked God to approve his words and thoughts as though they were offerings brought to God's altar. He ended this thought in Psalm 19 with a prayer that God might be pleased with his words. As you begin this day—and each day—remember to ask God to guide what you say and what you think. David prayed,

> *Let the words of my mouth*
> *and the meditation of my heart*
> *be acceptable in Your sight,*
> *O Lord, my rock and my Redeemer.*
> (Psalm 19:14)

14

Walking in Obedience —Confidence—

In the fear of the LORD *there is strong confidence,*
and his children will have refuge.
PROVERBS 14:26

A Prayer to Pray—

Dear compassionate Lord, Your mercies have brought me to the dawn of a new day. Through Your grace move my will to respond to Your wisdom, for the power to obey is not in me, but in Your freely given love alone which enables me to serve You. May this be a day when I, in holy awe, progress toward greater obedience to Your perfect will. Amen.

Growing up in Oklahoma, tornadoes and their destructive powers were a constant and eminent threat. Every time a storm rolled across the plains, my family and I would stand outside and look at the sky with concern and caution—and utter awe. Were we afraid? No...well, maybe a little...as long as the storm was at a distance! But the best description of our emotions was one of respect. We knew those storms were capable of producing great devastation—even death. Out of regard for their potential for destruction, we had our family plan, practiced our plan for survival, and followed through on that plan at the first hint of a tornado.

Our concern or possibly fear was out of respect for the power of those violent disturbances of nature. The native American Indians who lived in earlier times in that very same area of Oklahoma possibly had worshipped such storms, considering their power as something awesome and divine.

Here in Proverbs 14 we again read the phrase "the fear of the LORD" (Proverbs 14:2,26-27). This phrase first appeared in Proverbs 1:7 when the subject of knowledge and wisdom was introduced—"The fear of the LORD is the beginning of knowledge." It has appeared again and again, and by the time you finish reading through the book of Proverbs, it will have appeared more than 15 times.[1] This amount of repetition and emphasis on "the fear of the Lord" is a red alert to us of the magnitude of its importance.

Understanding the Fear of the Lord

Because the phrase "the fear of the Lord" is used three times in this chapter of Proverbs, let's try to get a better understanding of what it means to "fear the Lord." The fear I had and still have for the kinds of storms that occurred in Oklahoma is not one of hysterical, uncontrolled panic, but one of enormous respect. I understand the potential for total destruction to any and all people and property that is in the path of such a storm. I respect or honor the storm by taking precautions when one is looming on the horizon.

Bible scholars have affirmed that this is the way we should approach the phrase "the fear of the Lord." Because of who God is and His almighty power over all things, we honor Him and show reverence and respect by being obedient to His will. We are awed by God and in awe of Him. This kind of reverence or reverential fear should be the controlling influence in our lives. When it is, and when we honor God, our lives will be blessed and will take on a number of qualities, such as:

Those who fear the Lord have integrity—"He who walks in his uprightness fears the LORD, but he who is devious in his ways despises Him" (Proverbs 14:2). Walking in "uprightness" or integrity is an outward demonstration of what it means to "fear" or honor God in our heart and daily life choices. Following the way that is opposite to uprightness—the devious, perverse, or crooked way—is an outward demonstration of what it means to disregard and dishonor and disrespect the Lord. A person cannot say they honor and respect and worship God if they are walking in disobedience—if they are lacking integrity. Jesus put it this way: "If you love Me, you will keep My commandments" (John 14:15).

Those who fear the Lord have confidence—"In the fear of the LORD there is strong confidence, and his children will have refuge" (Proverbs 14:26). Notice where confidence is placed—"in the fear of the Lord." This kind of confidence should always be a part of our lives. But when we are disobedient to the ways of the Lord—when we fail to fear, revere, respect, obey, and follow Him—doubt and fear move in, and our confidence in our relationship with God and our position in His family is shaken and weakens and crumbles.

This is exactly what happened in the garden of Eden. Adam and Eve walked with God, talked with God, and enjoyed unbroken fellowship with God…until they chose to disobey Him. Suddenly, they noticed they were naked. They had never before avoided God, but they now found themselves looking for a good hiding place!

Doubt and hesitation instantly arose in Adam and Eve after they willfully disobeyed God in the garden. Their fellowship with God was broken. Instead of walking in the coolness of the garden *with* God, they hid from Him. When confronted by God, Adam confessed, "I heard the sound of You in the garden, and I was afraid…so I hid myself" (Genesis 3:10).

When you have your priorities in order, and when your heart is focused on obeying and pleasing the Lord, and when you are walking by the Spirit, you will not be running away from God. No, you will cherish and cling to Him—secure, safe, and cherished by Him. You will experience the peace of God in Your heart. As Proverbs 18:10 says, "The name of the LORD is a strong tower; the righteous runs into it and is safe." A preacher summarized the fear of the Lord in these words: "Men who fear God face life fearlessly. Men who do not fear God end up fearing everything."[2]

I hope you caught the second part—the ending words—of our primary verse: "In the fear of the LORD there is strong confidence, *and his children will have refuge*" (Proverbs 14:26). Everyone is blessed if they have a place of refuge when life gets threatening. Not only is God your refuge, but as you are faithful to turn to Almighty God, pray to Him, and rely on Him, you are showing others how to handle fear and stress.

Those who fear the Lord are on the path to wisdom—"The fear of the Lord is the instruction for wisdom, and before honor comes humility" (Proverbs 15:33). This proverb makes it clear that "the fear of the Lord is not merely the gateway but the whole path of wisdom."[3] Having a lifestyle and attitude that fears the Lord becomes the means by which God trains us in His ways—the ways of wisdom. Here's a short list of good things that come from fearing the Lord:

- Fear of the Lord directs our use of wisdom.
- Fear of the Lord reminds us that understanding and knowledge are gifts to be used for the benefit of others.
- Fear of the Lord never allows us to forget who God is, and that we aren't God.
- Fear of the Lord fosters the right kind of humility.

> The finest honors we receive in life are wasted if they aren't preceded by humility and if they don't proceed from our use of wisdom to make a difference in people's lives.[4]

Those who fear the Lord think like God—"The fear of the Lord is to hate evil; pride and arrogance and the evil way and the perverted mouth, I hate" (Proverbs 8:13). Throughout the book of Proverbs, the thoughts and actions of wisdom parallel godly thinking. Here in Proverbs 8:13, God is saying that those who follow Him—those who "fear the Lord"—will hate evil, just as He hates attitudes and sins like pride and arrogance, the perverted mouth, and the evil way. To fear the Lord and to think like the Lord, we must ask ourselves, "Do I hate evil like God hates evil, or have I become thick-skinned and am accepting society's evils as part of everyday life?" Our goal as followers of God is to think and act like Him, and that involves the fear of the Lord. "The fear of the Lord is a state of mind in which one's own attitudes, will, feelings, deeds, and goals are exchanged for God's."[5]

God's Wisdom...for Your Day

As a woman, I fight fear on a daily basis. Prayer and the promises of God are my daily bread! Who isn't afraid of crime? Jim and I have experienced two break-ins and burglaries, so our safety at home is a matter of constant prayer to trust God rather than fear what man can do to us (Psalm 56:4). And who isn't afraid of harm or suffering to ourselves or our loved ones? Yes, we've had the dreaded "Dad, I've been in a car wreck" call. We've also been through cancer with one of our daughters and serious health and physical issues with several grandchildren.

Like you, for these and all other fears, we have our loving Father to run to and find shelter in the shadow of the Almighty. He is our strong tower! Our strength. Our refuge. He constantly watches over us, His children. Praise Him constantly for His constant watch-care. Trust Him daily for His loving provision and guidance. Turn to Him with your heart's first flutter of fear. Lean on Him. And love Him with all your heart, soul, mind, and strength.

And "fear" Him. The word "fear" when applied to God and the fear of the Lord is a good thing. Over and over again, we see this "fear" as a positive attitude toward God. We could call this attitude "God-consciousness." This "fear of the Lord" means you and I acknowledge God's sovereignty and are aware of His presence in every area of our life. No part of our life is off limits, overlooked, or ignored by God. The fear of the Lord means we seek to obey Him in all things and respond to Him with our wholehearted obedience.

The book of Proverbs says multiple times in multiple proverbs and in multiple ways that when you have a sold-out attitude toward God, you will experience the many rich blessings of God. And those blessings won't stop with you. Your friends and family will receive the first overflow of your God-centered heart and lifestyle. As the verse for this chapter observes, "In the fear of the LORD there is strong confidence, and his children will have refuge" (Proverbs 14:26). God is your refuge, He is your family's refuge, and He always will be. As one translation reads, "Those who fear the LORD are secure; he will be a place of refuge for their children."[6]

When you fear the Lord, you are blessed to be a blessing to others. Anyone who gets near you—starting with, and especially, your family—will also be blessed. Through any threat or storm—or tornado!—or suffering or sorrow, you have a powerful strength you can give to others. Give that gift of strength freely and daily.

Today set your "self" aside, reach out, and bless others. Share with them the knowledge of God's blessing of love and redemption through Jesus Christ. Pray that your loved ones and others you share with will also come to love and fear the Lord—to possess strong confidence and to have a refuge in God, who is a very present help in time of need.

God is our refuge and strength,
a very present help in trouble.
(Psalm 46:1)

15

Enjoying the Benefits of Wisdom
—Choices—

A gentle answer turns away wrath,
but a harsh word stirs up anger.
The tongue of the wise makes knowledge acceptable,
but the mouth of fools spouts folly.
PROVERBS 15:1-2

A Prayer to Pray—

O God of all wisdom, knowing that You have done all things well and Your work in my behalf is perfect, help me approach this new day, seeking Your perfect will for each decision and choice I make. Today may my delight be to do Your will, my Rock and my salvation. Amen.

Before profiling became a science in assessing a person's habits, principles, beliefs, and views, the book of Proverbs already contained lists and labels for certain types of people or personalities. So far in Proverbs you have encountered the profiles of the fool and the wise person. You've noted the marks of those who are evil versus the righteous. You've seen what God has to say about those who are lazy sluggards and those who are diligent. And you have observed those who lie contrasted with those who value the truth.

Everyone—including you and me—has their own unique profile. Hopefully, as we enter Proverbs 15, you will be blessed and challenged by the profile of the character qualities that are a part of the makeup of a woman of wisdom who chooses wisely.

Life Is Full of Choices

I am extremely excited about chapter 15 of Proverbs because it is so valuable to women who long to be wise and live in a way that glorifies God. As in the other "contrasting" proverbs (Proverbs 10–14), you can't help but notice the profound contrasts in the behavior of the wise woman or person, and the foolish woman or person.

Here's a little trivia as we consider the study of wisdom and folly. I hesitate even writing about fools and foolish behavior because I've definitely been there and done that! In some ways, this will be like looking in a mirror for me—and maybe most women. Even though it may be painful, let's link arms and do this together. Hopefully and prayerfully, when we are finished, we will both be more likely to act wisely at the next opportunity, which will most definitely come sooner, not later!

For your information, in the book of Proverbs the word "wise" occurs 64 times while "fool" occurs 76 times. "Foolish" occurs

18 times, and "wisdom" 49 times. In many of these proverbs, the wise and foolish are contrasted. I couldn't help but see these contrasts as I read Proverbs 15 on my monthly reading schedule. A look at this chapter and a few proverbs from chapter 14 will reveal more about wise choices versus foolish ones. Keep in mind what your personal profile looks like today—and discover ways to improve it to look more like *God's* profile of a wise woman.

A wise woman's words have a positive effect—"A gentle answer turns away wrath, but a harsh word stirs up anger. The tongue of the wise makes knowledge acceptable, but the mouth of fools spouts folly" (Proverbs 15:1-2). These two proverbs give us tremendous advice.

First, we learn that by choosing self-control and a gentle manner, we can turn an opponent into an advocate (verse 1). When someone is angry, argumentative, or furious, that's our cue to use or answer with words that are the opposite. That's a signal for us to choose and carefully select words that are soft, gentle, pleasant, mild, and calming.

Like water on a fire, your sweet, softly spoken words cool and settle a person's soul. They quell the out-of-control emotions in another. In my mind I picture an agitated, fussy baby or toddler who is confused, rigid, writhing, and screaming—who's having a fit! And along comes mom, cooing, whispering, and soothing her child while she wraps her baby in a blanket and coddles and soothes him or her into a quiet state.

Imagine the ministry your "gentle answer" has in an unpleasant scene, in the face of anger. Master the grace of a gentle answer when dealing with people's emotions, and start at home. As another translation reads, "A gentle answer is a quarrel averted."[1]

Our proverb also shows us that negative responses and results are always a possibility. If, instead of answering with a soft, gentle answer, you respond with a harsh, inflamed, stinging word, you can make a harsh enemy.

Verse 18 gives similar advice: "A hot-tempered man stirs up strife, but the slow to anger calms a dispute." The choice—and often the outcome—is up to you. Will you speak and act as a hothead, or as a peacemaker? A hothead becomes a storm center, while a peacemaker "carries about with them an atmosphere in which quarrels die a natural death."[2]

A wise woman builds—"The wise woman builds her house, but the foolish tears it down with her own hands" (Proverbs 14:1). In this chapter we are focusing on the benefits of wisdom, and here we see yet another choice you and I must make. The choice is basically, Do I want to build or destroy my home?

This verse is not speaking of literal house construction, but of home building. It tells us a wise woman spends the time necessary to create a happy and comfortable place for herself and her family to live and others to enjoy. The ultimate picture of the efforts of this wise woman who "builds her house" is found in Proverbs 31:10-31.

A foolish woman, however, tears down "with her own hands" whatever home life she has. Unfortunately, our words, neglect, laziness, anger, and lack of self-control can, day by day and little by little, tear down and destroy a home and family. Make this your homemaking goal: "She looks well to the ways of her household" (Proverbs 31:27).

A wise woman's speech is not inflammatory—"In the mouth of the foolish is a rod for his back, but the lips of the wise will protect them" (Proverbs 14:3). This proverb could be translated, "Words can come back to roost." How often have you said something and, the second you said it, you knew it was going to come back to haunt you? And sure enough, those very words got you into a world of trouble and sorrow! But a wise woman who guards her heart and her lips tries hard not to say things that could later return in a negative way. What's the solution? Don't say anything you wouldn't want God to hear, and don't say anything that would hurt another person.

A wise woman chooses the company she keeps—"Leave the presence of a fool, or you will not discern words of knowledge" (Proverbs 14:7). You've probably heard the saying, "You are known by the company you keep." The writer of this proverb is saying that if you choose to hang around and spend time with foolish people, your behavior will begin to mirror their foolishness. You will soon become as foolish as they are and end up doing foolish things yourself—becoming a fool yourself! The solution? Stay away from foolish people! Have nothing to do with them. Get away from them quickly—as soon as possible! As this proverb screams, "*Leave* the presence of a fool."

A wise woman is careful—"The wisdom of the sensible is to understand his way, but the foolishness of fools is deceit" (Proverbs 14:8). Other translations use the word "prudent" to describe this sensible woman who knows what she must do and knows how to behave. She considers her actions. She thinks before she acts. She "is cautious and turns away from evil" (verse 16). The foolish woman, however, does not think first because she is convinced she already knows everything. She fails to seek out what God has to say about her situation and fails to seek the counsel of others. As a woman who must wade through tough issues and decisions every day, you need to depend on God-given wisdom to know how best to proceed in each circumstance and with every encounter.

A wise woman is not boastful—"Wisdom rests in the heart of one who has understanding, but in the hearts of fools it is made known" (Proverbs 14:33). A wise woman does not parade her knowledge. She doesn't have to! She is confident in her relationship with God and comfortable in what she knows of His Word and how He wants her to live. Wisdom rests easily within her heart and soul, and she has no need to boast about what she knows in front of others. A foolish woman, however, loves to parade the little she knows before others. It is the act of boasting that gives her away as a fool. As another proverb puts it, "Even a fool, when he keeps silent, is considered wise; when he closes his lips, he is considered prudent" (17:28). I keep this verse on my bathroom mirror as a reminder to think before I speak! Yes, indeed! It is better to be thought a fool than to open your mouth and prove it.

God's Wisdom...for Your Day

This look at the importance of choices has been packed and full—and challenging! As Proverbs 14:8 stated, a sensible woman seeks to "understand [her] way." Let's do that now.

What is the pattern of your life? What is your profile looking like? Do your life, your actions, and your choices characterize you as a wise woman? If not, then you've got some rewarding work to do—the best kind of work. You can work on submitting to the Holy Spirit's transforming power. You can work on praying and seeking to live God's way. You can work on making good, better, and best choices—godly choices.

The rewards of becoming a wise woman are many and spectacular. We learned in Proverbs 4:9 that wisdom "will place on your head a garland of grace; she will present you with a crown of beauty." Then in Proverbs 14, verses 18 and 24, we read that "the sensible are crowned with knowledge" and "the crown of the wise is their riches."

The result of choosing to pursue wisdom is the reward of a "crown of knowledge" and a "crown of riches." Whether this refers to literal riches or to a beautiful, orderly life that comes from wise living, God's message is clear: The daily choices you make today determine the outcome of your days.

16

Believing Your Heavenly Father Knows Best

—Guidance—

The mind of man plans his way,
but the LORD directs his steps.
PROVERBS 16:9

A Prayer to Pray—

O Sovereign Father and guide for all who trust in You, the way is unclear and the future uncertain, but Your Word is a lamp to my feet and a guide for my path. May the light of Your grace shine brightly on this, my new day—a gift from You. May Your Holy Spirit guide me into all truth. Because You alone know what is best for me, with all my heart I ask You to help me today to remember Your Son's words: "Not My will, but Yours, be done." Amen.

As I've been attempting to read through my Bible every year, I have also tried to study specific books of the Bible with the help of Bible commentaries. I've always enjoyed the Psalms and delighted in spending time delving into them for more detailed study. As I shared in the introduction of this book, I still remember learning that if I wanted to know more about my relationship with God, I should read the book of Psalms, and if I wanted to know about my relationship with my fellow man, I should read the book of Proverbs.

After diving into a study of Proverbs, I must now amend my original thinking. The shift started when I read, "The fear of the LORD is the beginning of knowledge" (Proverbs 1:7). That's when I realized that Proverbs is a book as much about the theology of God as it is about personal interaction with my fellow man. Proverbs refers to the "Lord" over 90 times, and there are also multiple references to "the fear of the Lord."

And now, here in chapter 16, you will discover that God is very much interested in you! Proverbs 16 is loaded and packed full of advice. God desires to be involved in every aspect of your life. And praise His glorious name, He—the Father of wisdom, your heavenly Father—knows best!

What Your Heavenly Father Does for You

God always has the last word—"The plans of the heart belong to man, but the answer of the tongue is from the LORD" (Proverbs 16:1). You could state this principle another way: "You make your proposals—but God disposes." Balaam is a perfect example of a man trying to do something his way. Balaam was commissioned by a local king to curse God's people. When he opened his mouth to deliver the curses, not once, but twice, the words that came out of his mouth were a blessing instead (Numbers 23:7-10,18-24)! God overruled.

Here's another example of God's guidance: Jesus' disciples were worried about what they should say when they were tried for their faith. Jesus assured and encouraged them, "Do not worry about how or what you are to say; for it will be given you in that hour what you are to say" (Matthew 10:19). God would give them the proper words at the proper time. Psalm 37:5 says your job assignment is to "Commit your way to the Lord, trust also in Him." And God's job? "...and He will do it." What assurance!

Proverbs 10:24 also states, "The desire of the righteous will be granted." God wants you to set goals that aim at being a stronger Christian and a godly woman. He wants you to use some of your time serving others, and to be a faithful steward of your money. So make your plans. Put your dreams on paper. Take action—and trust in Him. When your heart's desire is to do His will, He will lead, guide, overrule, and redirect to bring His will to pass. What comfort!

God knows the intentions of your heart—"All the ways of a man are clean in his own sight, but the Lord weighs the motives" (Proverbs 16:2). Are you familiar with Jeremiah 17:9? Its message is similar: "The heart is more deceitful than all else and is desperately sick; who can understand it?" Even the most violent criminal rationalizes his sin to himself. And unfortunately, we are also able to think what we say and do is all right—that it's "clean." But when we measure our motives against God's standards, we realize the error of our ways. God is not fooled by our actions. He looks at our hearts—and He judges. When your motives are pure and clean, you are more likely to do what is right since pure motives usually produce right actions.

God honors the work that honors Him—"Commit your works to the Lord and your plans will be established" (Proverbs 16:3).

The best way to insure that your dreams and goals become reality is to dedicate or "commit" your work to the Lord from the beginning—to want only what He wants. Pray and seek His approval each day and with each step. As our proverb instructs, "Commit your works to the LORD."

If what you are attempting is God's work, in total trust roll the burden of your work onto the Lord. Commit your works to Him. While you may have some anxious moments, your burdens are never too great for Him to bear!

God has a purpose for everything—"The LORD has made everything for its own purpose, even the wicked for the day of evil" (Proverbs 16:4). Have you ever sung the perky little song, "Everything is beautiful in its own time"? It and Proverbs 16:4 are like Ecclesiastes 3:1, which tells us, "There is an appointed time for everything. And there is a time for every event under heaven." We should be joyfully singing this little tune and praising God that all is well and beautiful—no matter how it may look or feel. God has a purpose for everything—"even the wicked for the day of evil."

Each new day should bring you a thrill—God has a purpose for you! Thank Him with all your heart...then pray that your every action and attitude would glorify Him.

God has a plan for your life—"The mind of man plans his way, but the LORD directs his steps" (Proverbs 16:9). You simply cannot miss the point of this proverb: Man may make his plans, but...

> "the LORD directs his steps" (16:9),
> "the answer of the tongue is from the LORD" (16:1),
> and
> "every decision is from the LORD" (16:33).

Maybe you've gone to great lengths to plan your life and set goals for your career. And, hopefully, you have prayed and sought God's direction. However, if you are one of God's children, He is guiding your steps, whether you are aware of His guidance or not.

Maybe you've had an "Esther experience." Esther, a young Jewish woman in the Old Testament, had her personal plans and dreams, but God had other plans...which led her to become queen of the Persian Empire, placing her in a position to help save the Jewish race, God's people.

Trust God with your life and life plan. He always knows best. Hold nothing tightly and all things lightly. Why? God may have other plans—His plans!—for your future.

God is looking for honesty—"A just balance and scales belong to the LORD; all the weights of the bag are His concern" (Proverbs 16:11). Weights and measures are still very much a part of business and commerce. In years past, shop owners manipulated their bag of weights in order to make additional profit. This proverb is all about honesty. There are a multitude of ways to be dishonest. Even with all our laws, the government can't keep people from cheating. But for you and me, God is wanting us to submit to His higher standard in all areas and at all levels, even when we go to the supermarket!

God rewards those who seek Him—"He who gives attention to the word will find good, and blessed is he who trusts in the LORD" (Proverbs 16:20). Giving attention to "the word" means trusting God and His Word, His Scriptures, to guide and direct your life so you "find good" and are "blessed." I can't help but think of Jesus' words, "Blessed are those who hunger and thirst for righteousness, for they shall be satisfied" (Matthew 5:6).

Proverbs 16:20 sends us this message: Read your Bible, obey it, and trust the One who wrote it. You can't go wrong with this winning formula for living a victorious life!

God hears your prayers—"The LORD is far from the wicked, but He hears the prayer of the righteous" (Proverbs 15:29). Someone has estimated that there are 3000 promises in the Bible, but perhaps none is as encouraging or exciting as the promise that God hears your prayers! The Lord is far from the wicked in the sense that He does not enter into fellowship with them, and they are not in touch with Him by prayer. But as a believer, by prayer you have access to an instant 24/7 audience with the Sovereign God of the universe—right before His very throne in heaven! And here's another truth and a promise: "We know that God does not hear sinners; but if anyone is God-fearing and does His will, He hears him" (John 9:31). If your heavenly Father knows best, and you have free access to Him, make sure prayer is an important part of your day. And here's yet another promise and truth to remember as you pray:

> *Therefore let us draw near with confidence to the throne of grace, so that we may receive mercy and find grace to help in time of need.*
> (Hebrews 4:16)

God's Wisdom...for Your Day

Does it bother you that God is sovereign? That He is in control of the universe and actively involved in the lives of His children, including you? If so, think about this: How do you show your loved ones that you care? You do it by being involved in their lives, right? Even when they don't want your involvement, you do what you can to be there for those you love.

God is no different. In fact, His concern never wavers or ceases. Because your heavenly Father knows what's best, He guides and directs your life. No one is better qualified to give you that wisdom and guidance. Today and every day make it a practice to thank God and acknowledge His love for you, His presence in your life, and His guidance. Commit your day and your plan to Him and trust Him to guide you into His perfect will.

Trust in the LORD *with all your heart*
and do not lean on your own understanding.
In all your ways acknowledge Him,
and He will make your paths straight.
(Proverbs 3:5-6)

17

Being a Good Friend
—Friendship—

A friend loves at all times,
and a brother is born for adversity.
PROVERBS 17:17

A Prayer to Pray—

God in heaven above, as You spoke face-to-face to Your friend Moses in the past, and as Your Son came to earth to be the friend of sinners, may I be a faithful friend to others. My heart's desire is to follow in Your steps and be a friend who covers transgressions, who is loyal in times of adversity, who seeks to love unconditionally, and who can be trusted without question. Help me be honest with my friends when I need to speak up, and not to forget to pray for the spiritual health and growth of my treasured friends. Amen.

What would we do without our friends! From the time we began kindergarten and grade school and throughout the remainder of our lives, every woman looks for and needs friends. God has made us social beings because we are created in the image of God (Genesis 1:26). This means we resemble God in some very special ways, and one of those ways is that, like God, we are social beings.

First and foremost, we were created to have fellowship with God. Of course, God doesn't need us as friends, but He chose to be our friend and to fellowship with us through His Son, Jesus Christ (John 15:14-15). But God also created us to have fellowship with our fellow man. This is where the book of Proverbs comes to our rescue because it is a guidebook to having, managing, and keeping up relationships with those around us.

The Proof of a Good Friend

Proverbs 17 is one of my favorites because it tells us what it means to be a friend. This is key because to have friends, you have to be a friend. And let's go one step further and say this: To have the right kind of friends means you have to be the right kind of friend. Here are a few vital marks of being a good friend. These marks are the proof and evidence that you are a true friend.

A good friend is forgetful—"He who conceals a transgression seeks love, but he who repeats a matter separates intimate friends" (Proverbs 17:9). Overlooking or forgiving an offense goes a long way in preserving a friendship. I love this scenario between Jesus and Peter when Peter asked, "Lord, how often shall my brother sin against me and I forgive him? Up to seven times?" Jesus, our Savior who forgives all our sins, then patiently explained to Peter that our forgiveness should be limitless: "Up to seventy times seven" (Matthew 18:21-22).

Here's how this proverb works:

> One woman says to another: "Don't you remember the mean things she said to you?"
>
> The other woman replies: "I not only don't remember; I distinctly remember forgetting!"

When the Bible says "As far as the east is from the west, so far has He removed our transgressions from us" (Psalm 103:12), it means God has forgiven our sin and will remember it no more. He forgives—and forgets, and we are to model His forgiveness—and His forgetting. These people in the Bible show us the beauty of forgiveness:

- Joseph forgave his brothers who sold him into slavery in a foreign country...so their family could be reunited and dwell together in peace and their numbers could increase and become a mighty nation.
- Paul forgave John Mark, who turned away and left Paul and his mission team...so later they could serve the Lord together.
- Sarah must have forgiven Abraham, who endangered her life when he lied, saying she was only his sister...so their marriage could move forward.

In all three of these scenarios, a terrible wrong was committed, and faithful people suffered and were put in jeopardy. Once forgiveness was extended, in every case something positive was accomplished.

A good friend is loyal—"A friend loves at all times, and a brother is born for adversity" (Proverbs 17:17). This proverb tells us that a true friend can be counted on like a family member—through the good times...and the bad. In fact, according to Proverbs 18:24, this loyal friend actually "sticks closer than a brother." Family may band together when there is a family crisis, but friends are actually closer than family because they have a daily, close role in a friend's life. Their love is constant. In other words, when you hang in there and go through adversity with a friend, you prove you are not a "fair weather" friend. As a good friend who is loyal, you are there when a friend needs you. Sure, friendship takes time—lots of it!—and a friend's needs almost never come at a convenient time. But a good friend is loyal, truehearted, and steady as a rock, especially during adversity—they are present, praying, caring, helping, calling, crying, faithfully providing whatever is needed.

The original readers of this proverb did not know Jesus and His teachings, but we know today how loyal our friend Jesus is. In His own words, He assures us, "I give eternal life to them, and they will never perish; and no one shall snatch them out of My hand" (John 10:28). Now, that's true friendship! Be sure to notice the word "never." And now notice it again in this second promise from Jesus: "I will never leave you nor forsake you" (Hebrews 13:5 NKJV). And here's an "always" to note, to remember, and to hold in your heart: "I am with you always, even to the end of the age" (Matthew 28:20).

A good friend is not shallow—"A man of too many friends comes to ruin, but there is a friend who sticks closer than a brother" (Proverbs 18:24). Another version of the Bible translates this proverb to read, "There are friends who pretend to be friends, but there is a friend who sticks closer than a brother" (RSV). Indiscriminately choosing friends for a variety of motives can bring trouble. Who hasn't wanted to be a part of a clique, a member of a club, to be seen with the popular people? (If this sounds like middle and high school, that's because that's what I'm recalling from that stage of my life!) Rarely do these "shallow" desires turn out to reap positive results and for-real, lifelong friendships.

However, when you cultivate genuine friendships with genuine people, they will stick with you through thick and thin—and so will you with them. This is becoming more rare because of a culture that centers on social media. Maybe you have spent years developing 500 friends or followers on a social network. But what happens when you are sick and need a meal, or when you are crawling day by day through a tragedy or loss, when life gets serious? Which one of these "friends" can or would come to your aid? A better—far better—use of your precious time is to spend it on becoming friends with a few "real friends" who are not iffy and shallow, but are like a faithful sister.

Of course, with good, close, and best friends there's lots of fun and good times, celebrations, and coffee—and lunch!—and get-togethers. But good friends are never shallow with one another. Real friends pray together and for one another. They share spiritual truths and encourage each other's spiritual growth. They speak and talk of the Lord and what they are learning.

Authentic friends come alongside you when you are hurting or down or suffering. Whatever you need is given. Do you need a praying sister in Christ? Do you need a ride to the doctor because you're too sick to drive? Do you need a meal because you're unable to fix it yourself? Do you need some counsel about a personal matter? About a family issue? About a serious decision you must make? Whatever you need, your true friend will come to your aid—and you would do the same for her. It's almost like a real friend is always on standby, always available when you have a real need.

A good friend can be trusted—"A perverse man spreads strife, and a slanderer separates intimate friends" (Proverbs 16:28). The word "slanderer," which can be translated "words of a whisperer," occurs three other times in Proverbs (see Proverbs 18:8; 26:20,22). The opposite of a perverse, slandering whisperer is a good, for-real friend, someone you can tell anything to and know they will keep it to themselves. Gossip separates friends and also drives a wedge between others who are close friends.

Proverbs has a lot to say about gossip, slander, and an evil tongue. The quickest way to keep from being a "good" friend is to spread information or intimate facts about her or about another person. A good friend covers their friends with a cloak of love and protects their confidences at all costs. We've been examining what a genuine or real friendship is. To find, make, and be such a friend, be careful when you choose your friends. Keep this Spanish proverb in mind: "Whoever gossips *to* you will gossip *about* you."[1]

A good friend is an adviser—"Oil and perfume make the heart glad, so a man's counsel is sweet to his friend" (Proverbs 27:9). This proverb pictures good friends in the role of cheering up one another. Amazingly, the proverb says your loving advice should encourage and delight the hearer in the way that taking a bubble bath refreshes the body!

Elizabeth was this kind of friend and adviser when her young, unwed, pregnant cousin Mary came for a visit (Luke 1:39-56). The two of them shared, prayed, and exalted the Lord together. Jonathan was also this kind of friend when he strengthened David in the Lord. Jonathan, whose father was trying to kill

David, risked his life to meet with David to "encourage him in God." Jonathan reminded David of God's promises, and he assured David, "I will be next to you" (1 Samuel 23:16-17).

Besides being a friend who reassures your friends, you are also to brace, steady, and sharpen them as Proverbs says in 27:17: "Iron sharpens iron, so one man sharpens another." Just as the action of iron against iron sharpens, so the interchange of ideas you have with your close friends should sharpen their thinking. You are not being a good friend if you only talk about the weather and the latest TV shows and news or Hollywood gossip.

No, you are not to be a woman who pulls your friends down or merely along. You are to be a friend who pulls your friends up—up toward God, up in godliness, up in character, up in ministry and service to others. The perfect, most logical—and powerful—place to start your ministry of encouraging your friends is with sharing scriptures from the Bible. God will be honored, what you share will be truth, and you and your friend will be growing upward together in the Lord.

God's Wisdom...for Your Day

There's no doubt that being a good, true, honest, loving, and faithful friend is important to God. It's an essential part of His plan for your life. Friends and friendships begin with you, and to have the right kind of friends starts with you having the highest standards for yourself. If you deeply and passionately love God, it will be manifested by your life. It will show. It will be obvious. It will be seen—and heard, "for out of the abundance of the heart [the] mouth speaks" (Luke 6:45 NKJV). Live for God and, like a magnet, He will draw godly people into your life who will be the kind of friends you can encourage—and who will also encourage you.

I'm sure your days are busy, packed, hectic, and challenging. The temptation is always present to see what we can *not* do today in order to take care of the biggies—home, family, job, and church responsibilities. It's easy to let your friend category go...for just one day. Then at the end of your week, friends were neglected and overlooked for an entire week!

When I reached this stage, I made a few simple changes. I prayed each day for what I called my "Five Faithful Friends." Each day I also reached out to communicate with one of them in some way—even if I had to leave a voice mail. It only took a handful of minutes! Maybe you can do the same with your friends, or think of other ways to be a caring friend from under your personal pile of obligations. The apostle Paul prayed for his friends in faraway Philippi—and he wrote them letters. What kept him going? What kept him reaching out? What kept him trying to stay in touch? In his own words, Paul said, "...because I have you in my heart" (Philippians 1:7).

This is where your friends belong—in your heart.

18

Finding Something Good —A Wife After God's Own Heart—

He who finds a wife finds a good thing
and obtains favor from the LORD.
PROVERBS 18:22

A Prayer to Pray—

Glorious and Holy God, as I come before Your throne of grace and mercy, I acknowledge and praise Your forgiveness in Christ, my Savior. Knowing that I have a choice each day to bring honor or dishonor to my husband, help me make choices throughout this day that honor and show respect for my husband. Help me, dear Lord, to do him good and not evil today and all the days of my life. Amen.

In the ancient world, part of the significance of being a king was having multiple wives. The greater the king, the greater was the number of his wives! Solomon was the greatest king of his day, and he validated his might with 700 wives and 300 concubines (1 Kings 11:3).

The ordinary Israelite, however, seldom resorted to polygamy. Proverbs—a book of ancient wisdom—clearly shows that the union of one man with one woman was the norm and not the exception. Proverbs also takes the uncommon view held in ancient times that a wife was more than chattel and not solely for bearing children. Proverbs views a wife as her husband's companion, as a joy and a blessing: "Let your fountain be blessed, and rejoice in the wife of your youth" (Proverbs 5:18). A wife was also to be protected from physical danger according to this warning: "Whoever touches her will not go unpunished" (6:29).

Knowing God's exalted view of marriage, how should we view our role of wife as seen through the eyes of the writers of Proverbs? Read on.

A wife is a gift from God—"He who finds a wife finds a good thing and obtains favor from the LORD" (Proverbs 18:22). Acknowledging man's need, God created woman—a wife—for Adam. God declared, "It is not good for the man to be alone; I will make him a helper suitable for him" (Genesis 2:18).

Do you think of yourself as a gift God Himself has given to your husband, as "a good thing" that blesses your husband's life each day? Like any gift, you are special, unique, and given to your husband to bring him joy and happiness and, if God wills, to bear his children and extend his name to another generation.

A prudent wife is a godsend—"House and wealth are an inheritance from fathers, but a prudent wife is from the LORD"

(Proverbs 19:14). A husband can inherit real estate and money from his parents and relatives, but only the Lord can enable you to be a wife that is "prudent"—a wife that is careful, modest, sensible, restrained, and pleasant. In your moment by moment conduct as well as for the lifetime of your marriage, you are meant to be a "good gift"—a divine blessing—from God to your husband.

A wife of noble character is a crown—"An excellent wife is the crown of her husband, but she who shames him is like rottenness in his bones" (Proverbs 12:4). A king's crown sets him apart from commoners. In the same way, an excellent wife provides a crown for her husband, setting him apart from others who are not so fortunate.

To be a crown to your husband, make him your top priority. Put him as #1 on your to-do list, #1 on the list of people you admire and respect and want to spend time with. Make it clear to him that he can count on you for support and encouragement. Regarding her husband and marriage, an excellent wife "does him good and not evil all the days of her life" (31:12). As the saying goes, "Behind every successful man is a supportive wife." That's the message of this proverb. It gives you a glimpse into the value you can be to your husband. When your husband knows he can trust you and count on you for support and encouragement, the two of you can accomplish great results and lasting success in multiple areas and undertakings. Like child-raising. Serving in the church. Witnessing to your family members and neighbors. By creating and maintaining a loving home environment that welcomes any and all.

The opposite is also true: When a wife is at odds with her husband, or acts in ways that bring him shame, she becomes like a cancer or a physical disease that eats away at the marriage and spoils the fabric of the family unit. She, as Proverbs 12:4 says, "is like rottenness in his bones." With each new sunrise, you and I have a choice to make: to be a wife who blesses and brings honor and respect to her husband, or one whose behavior damages him and his reputation—and even his health.

A wife can make her home heaven on earth or a living hell—"The contentions of a wife are a constant dripping" (Proverbs 19:13). The poor man pictured in this proverb has a life sentence with a contentious, nagging wife. In our study of the wives portrayed in Proverbs, we now know that we can be a blessing and a crown to our husbands. But unfortunately, we can easily slip into the habit of being a contentious, nagging, complaining, demeaning wife who is disruptive, argumentative, quarrelsome, and wears her husband down day after day.

As an old Arab proverb notes, "Three things make a house intolerable: the leaking through of rain, a wife's nagging, and bugs."[1] Yet another commentator writes, "The 'constant dripping' of the complaining woman reminds us of the ancient Chinese water torture."[2]

To make sure we get the message, God adds additional proverbs about the awful "contentious woman." They speak for themselves. And I must warn you, this woman is not a pretty sight. She does not honor God, and she surely doesn't honor her husband! She is the bearer of torture and great misery.

> *It is better to live in a corner of a roof*
> *than in a house shared with a contentious woman.*
> (Proverbs 21:9)

> *It is better to live in a desert land*
> *than with a contentious and vexing woman.*
> (Proverbs 21:19)

It is better to live in a corner of the roof
than in a house shared with a contentious woman.
(Proverbs 25:24)

A constant dripping on a day of steady rain
and a contentious woman are alike.
(Proverbs 27:15)

The choice is ours: We can choose to delight in building up our man, or we can act like a grown-up mean girl who willfully tears down and wears down her life mate.

An excellent wife is for real—"An excellent wife, who can find?" Well, she's real and she's out there! I'm not one of those people who picks up a book and flips to the end to see if I want to read the book. But I can't help but have you read the end of the book of Proverbs for a preview and sneak peek at the Proverbs 31 woman, wife, and mother. Yes, this magnificent, noble wife is out there...and she's priceless: "For her worth is far above jewels" (Proverbs 31:10). This proverb reminds us of Proverbs 8:11, which speaks of wisdom as being "better than jewels; and all desirable things cannot compare with her."

God repeatedly states that wisdom is the ultimate commodity. Its value is beyond estimation. It is the key to life and godliness. God is letting you and me and all His readers know that the worth of a noble wife is second only to wisdom.

Look now at some of the positive character qualities in an excellent wife that are described in chapter 31:

- A "good wife" is a gift from God to bring her husband joy and happiness.
- A "prudent wife" whose behavior is godly is careful not to dishonor or disgrace her husband.

- A "virtuous" wife who possesses strength of character is a crowning possession.
- An "excellent wife" is worth more than jewels.

According to Proverbs 31:10-31, this excellent, virtuous, noble, devoted-to-her-family woman is a capable administrator and trader, a crafts-woman, philanthropist, and guide. Her home is the focus of her activities, yet her influence spreads far and wide. Her character and achievements are valued by her husband and children and by all who know of her. This woman is God's model for you and me as women, wives, and moms. Ask God to work in your life to make you a woman of noble character—a crown and a blessing to your husband and children.

God's Wisdom...for Your Day

Proverbs shows us the good, the bad, and the ugly qualities that can describe a wife. Yet God gives us the power to be a true gift from God, to bring good and do good in our marriage, to create a home that is a little heaven on earth. But we have the power through sin to ruin our marriage, to turn our marriage and home into a torturous hell, and to bring ruin to our husband. And the most frightening and sobering truth is that it's our choice which kind of wife we want to be—and will be.

As God's child you have the indwelling Holy Spirit who will guide you into all truth. He will produce in you His fruit of the Spirit as you walk in obedience to Him. You can oh so subtly slip into nagging, whining, complaining, arguing, and criticizing until, over time, you actually become a "contentious" wife. Or you can daily aspire to be the excellent, noble, virtuous, worthy wife God describes and exalts in Proverbs.

Today as you pray and pay attention to yourself as a wife and to your husband as someone precious whom God asks you to "love" (Titus 2:4), choose to be God's kind of wife. Choose to put your husband first. Choose to bless him, nurture him, build him up, and help him—to love him to pieces. Open your soul and pray for him and his day. Open your heart and love him with Christ's love. Open your eyes and see him as God's perfect gift to you. Open your mouth and praise him for his strengths and diligence. Open your hands and tend to his care and needs. Open your arms and embrace him as your teammate and leader, your best friend, your partner for life.

Make your marriage a good thing.

19

Conquering Your Worst Enemy —Anger—

A man of great anger shall bear the penalty,
for if you rescue him,
you will only have to do it again.
PROVERBS 19:19

A Prayer to Pray—

God, I bow before You, the God of all peace, who sent Your Son, the Prince of Peace, as a perfect role model of peace and patience. I thank and praise You that You give me clear instructions to put away anger, and helpful instructions for doing so, for gaining victory over anger and wrath. As I think about this day and its busyness, I want—just for today, dear Lord—to walk in Your ways, to obey Your Word and be the person You speak of who holds back anger and whose calm heart calms others. Amen.[1]

One way we know the Bible was written by God is because it is utterly honest in the descriptions of its characters. Take Cain, for instance. Born of Adam and Eve, Cain was the first child ever to be born. This made him extremely special and important because he was the future of the human race. Yet we quickly witness a major flaw in Cain—he had an anger problem, which came to a head when God rejected his offering.

The Bible doesn't say why God refused Cain's offering, but it does record Cain's reaction: "So Cain became very angry and his countenance fell." God then admonished Cain to get his anger under control, to pull it together, asking, "Why are you angry? And why has your countenance fallen? If you do well, will not your countenance be lifted up? And if you do not do well, sin is crouching at the door; and its desire is for you, but you must master it" (see Genesis 4:3-7).

Rather than listen to God and obey Him and master his anger, Cain was angry with God for declining his offering. He was also angry with his brother because Abel's offering was accepted by God. Cain let his anger master him and "rose up against Abel his brother and killed him" (verse 8).

You already know that anger is a prominent problem everyone struggles with in daily life. But God is faithful! He tells us throughout His Word to conquer and control our anger, and He's given us instructions on how to do it. The book of Proverbs has much to say about "anger." For instance:

Anger is a reaction—"A fool's anger is known at once, but a prudent man conceals dishonor" (Proverbs 12:16). How thick is your skin? Some people are thin-skinned, allowing the slightest criticism or insult or disappointment to send them into a fit of rage. A hot-tempered woman is almost impossible to be around. Her anger is always just under the radar. One little blip and she detonates. Being in her presence is like walking through a minefield. She's like a powder keg capable of blowing sky high at the slightest provocation.

The "prudent" woman in Proverbs 12:6, however—the woman God wants us to be—is a woman of wisdom who practices restraint. She has the grace to wait before she speaks or reacts, to be careful with her response and words, and to ignore insults. It takes two to argue or fight, and the prudent woman will not stoop to giving up her dignity to participate in a fight.

By God's grace you can and are to show restraint. Set your heart on doing what God asks of you. Desire to do whatever He says. You can learn to wait and pray before you respond to someone's complaints, accusations, or insults. You can, in essence, turn the other cheek and pass over a transgression rather than dishonor yourself and God, whom you represent, by losing your dignity and reacting to the anger and actions of "a fool."

The best news of all is that God has already given you every resource you need to manage anger. His Spirit's patience, gentleness, and self-control are available to you when you call upon Him to help you manage and handle a tough emotional situation. He will enable you to respond His way: "She opens her mouth with wisdom, and on her tongue is the law of kindness" (Proverbs 31:26 NKJV).

Anger is a loss of control—"A fool always loses his temper, but a wise man holds it back" (Proverbs 29:11). This is a straightforward verse telling us we are "a fool" if and when we lose our temper. Have you ever "lost it" with someone? (I know my answer is a shame-filled yes.) If so, it means you gave in to anger and blew up rather than waiting on the Lord and holding back your anger. Even if no permanent damage was done, losing your temper was wrong. At the very moment you give in to anger and ignite, the Bible describes each of us as "a fool."

Thank the Lord, again there is help! God gives us His wisdom in His Word and definitely throughout the entire book of Proverbs. And He gives us hope because with His grace, wisdom, and strength we can wait. We can "hold it back"—hold anger back. We can keep our emotions in check—maybe even count to ten! And while we're waiting and holding anger back, we can turn our heart toward God. We can send up a quick on-the-spot prayer for patience and direction. We can ask God to help us keep our mouth shut! And we can trust that His patience and wisdom will help and guide us in His path of wisdom.

It's vital that we as women after God's own heart deal with anger issues. It's important that we learn what to do instead of losing our temper. And it's imperative that we pray each day—and throughout the day—to take action at the first spark of anger.

God commands us to put away anger. As this proverb states, "A fool *always* loses his temper." This is frightening because if we don't take action against anger, and if we don't put away anger, we will come to the point where we are a certified, full-fledged fool—a woman who always loses her temper.

One of my favorite verses that I keep close in my heart for managing emotions and holding back from anger is 1 Peter 3:4. In this verse, God tells us to put away anger, but He also tells us to put on "a gentle and quiet spirit, which is precious in the sight of God." "Gentle" means you don't cause a disturbance, and "quiet" means you don't respond to the disturbances caused by others. With God's wisdom and power, you *can* hold your anger back.

Anger is contagious—"Do not associate with a man given to

anger; or go with a hot-tempered man, or you will learn his ways and find a snare for yourself" (Proverbs 22:24-25). Anger and angry people are a poison that infects us when we are with them. It's impossible to be around an angry person for more than a few minutes before you start getting angry too! Whatever their problem or issue is, their anger soon creeps into your own viewpoint, emotions, actions, and language. You've learned a new bad behavior!

But God comes to our rescue with clear instructions beginning with the words, "Do not..." This proverb strongly advises against associating or making friendships with angry people. They will be a corrupting influence. It's easy and natural to "learn" the ways of a hot-tempered person and become trapped in the sin of anger. The New Testament version of the principle from this proverb is, "Do not be deceived: Bad company corrupts good morals" (1 Corinthians 15:33)!

Anger is a habit—"A man of great anger will bear the penalty, for if you rescue him, you will only have to do it again" (Proverbs 19:19). A habit is defined as an acquired behavior pattern regularly followed until it has become almost involuntary. There are good habits like exercise and eating properly, and there are bad habits like smoking, drinking, and drugs that cause serious health issues and endanger others. Anger, like anything else you do often, can become a habit. Anger is like an addiction that cannot be controlled.

The first step toward managing a problem in any addict's life is to admit they have a problem. To own up to it. To call it what it is and refuse to excuse it. Where does the truth of this proverb find you on the anger scale? If you have a problem with anger, admit it as sin. Acknowledge your anger as a heart issue. God clearly and repeatedly commands throughout the Bible that we are not to be angry but to put it away and be done with it.

You can approach your heavenly Father and ask Him to search your heart for the root of your anger. You can humbly and boldly ask God for His help and grace to deal with your anger. And don't fail to ask forgiveness from those who have been the target or recipient of your anger.

Anger is avoidable—"A gentle answer turns away wrath, but a harsh word stirs up anger" (Proverbs 15:1). Have you ever thought about taking a class or course in self-defense? And are you wondering, "Does she mean a class in martial arts?" Well, that might not be a bad thing! But I'm actually thinking about Proverbs 15:1. The best self-defense against anger is a gentle, gracious reply from you when harsh or cutting words are spoken. When you give a gracious response, the first good thing that happens is you are not responding in anger—which would be sin—and two wrongs never make a right. And the second good thing that happens is you are not adding fuel to another person's anger. Remember: It take two to have an argument. Follow the advice of this little poem:

> Help me guard my lips, O Savior—
> Keep me sweet when sorely tried;
> Answers "soft" to others giving,
> Meekly "swallowing my pride."[2]

Anger is a decision—"A man's discretion makes him slow to anger, and it is his glory to overlook a transgression" (Proverbs 19:11). This proverb points out the "glory" (meaning beauty as an adornment) of self-control and its benefits as compared to the sure fallout and destruction caused by outbursts of anger. The Bible teaches us that anger (other than righteous anger) is wrong and self-defeating. More importantly, God tells us anger is sin. Therefore, nothing good can come from anger. Anger results in bad consequences and can produce hurt feelings, severed relationships, physical abuse—and more.

A woman of discretion—a woman with good sense—knows how to control her temper. She knows and agrees with God's Word that anger is sin. She has learned to be "slow to anger" and not give in to anger and blowups. She has discovered, as this proverb tells us, to humbly and graciously "overlook a transgression" when someone wrongs her.

When you show patience toward others and decide "to overlook a transgression," you are acting like God as you choose to demonstrate mercy and pity and extend grace toward others. You don't have to go to the mat in confrontation over every little thing or "transgression." Daily life is not a debate class or a physical sporting match. Instead, you can pray for the transgressor. You can in mercy and compassion wonder, *What's going on in her life? What would make her act like this, talk like this, say this?*

Remember, two wrongs never make a right. If someone provokes you (their wrong), you can fight back, argue, and accuse (your wrongs)...or you can gloriously, graciously let it go. Choose your battles. Very few things in your life are worth a war.

God's Wisdom...for Your Day

As you approach your fresh, new day, realize that it is a day your heavenly Father wants you to live as a representative for Him. It is also a day that will include numerous trials and temptations which can cause anger to surface. As you pray your opening "good morning prayer" to God, tell

Him your desire to not give in to anger today. Ask Him for His help and grace. And talk with Him minute by minute, task by task, and through each and every trial, surprise, difficult encounter, change in plans, and failure. Your goal is—just for today—not to give in to anger.

Anger is a dangerous emotion that is always hovering just under the surface. As God warned Cain, "Sin is crouching at the door; and its desire is fo...r you, but you must master it." My friend, the sin of anger is crouching at *your* door; its desire is for you, to have you, to control you. But, as God instructed, you can and must master anger (Genesis 4:7) by—

- getting rid of anger (Colossians 3:8 and Ephesians 4:31-32),
- keeping yourself under control (Proverbs 29:11),
- being quick to hear, slow to speak, and slow to become angry (James 1:19-20),
- responding with a soft, gentle answer (Proverbs 15:1), and
- looking to God for His fruit of the Spirit—patience and self-control (Galatians 5:22-23).

20

Getting All the Advice You Can —Counsel—

Prepare plans by consultation,
and make war by wise guidance.
PROVERBS 20:18

A Prayer to Pray—

I bow before You, Lord, recognizing that difficult times will come my way, and problems arise every day. I truly want to handle today's challenges Your way—in a godly manner. I am asking for Your help today—to not ignite and react to people and problems but to pause before You and seek to act as You teach me in Your Word. You have instructed me to not lean on my own understanding, but to acknowledge and look to You for guidance—and I bless You that You have promised You will direct my path. This, O Father, is what I desire today—to wait upon You and Your direction one step at a time, one trial at a time. With a heart of gratitude, I thank You! Amen.

It's fairly easy to receive advice when you don't know very much. But accepting advice is much harder when you think you know everything. Well, I have to report that as a baby Christian, seeking and taking in advice came easily because I knew I didn't know anything. In fact, I sought out wise and mature women who delighted in giving me direction in my roles as a woman. Their input and guidance launched my life as a Christian woman and has sustained me for the past four decades. This is true because what they shared with me was straight out of the Bible. It was God's Word—advice based on God's standards.

The Need for Good Advice

One problem with seeking advice is knowing there are two kinds of advice out there: good advice and bad advice...or what's worse—evil advice.

For instance, when Rehoboam became king, he asked advice from the elders of Israel—godly, seasoned men who had advised King Solomon, the wisest man of his day! Next, Rehoboam sought the opinions of the young men he had grown up with. In the end, King Rehoboam rejected the wisdom of the elders and took the foolish advice of his friends, buddies, and peers.

The result of the "bad" advice Rehoboam's not-so-wise friends gave him was epic: It led to the kingdom being torn apart, divided, and the two opposing groups going to war against one another (see 1 Kings 12:1-15).

The book of Proverbs makes it clear that the person who does not seek counsel is a fool. Proverbs also tells us the wise person is one who seeks counsel from the right people—from those who are wise: "The way of a fool is right in his own eyes, but a wise man is he who listens to counsel" (Proverbs 12:15).

Seven Steps of Wisdom

The book of Proverbs says repeatedly we should make it a habit to seek counsel before making a decision or doing something we might regret later. Like all Christians, you have and will face trials, emergencies, surprises, disappointments, setbacks, and tragedies of all sizes and about many matters.

Over time I have created what I refer to as "Seven Steps of Wisdom" for making my decisions. These seven steps come from God's Word. They were the result of learning from mistakes and bad decisions I made due to skipping one—or all!—of these steps. This list has since guided me every step of the way when I remember to follow it.

God has wisdom for every situation and every choice His people need to make. Following these steps will help you, too, to determine and accept the right kind of advice.

Step 1: Stop!

Generally, the first response most people make when something happens that's shocking, or hurtful, or an utter surprise is to react. Our natural tendency is to strike back, talk back, react, blow up, fall apart, cry, or throw our hands in the air and give up. Obviously, a first step toward wisdom is to realize that any of these reactions is our first hint that we are, or are close to, mishandling our situation!

So, before you do anything, just stop. And let me add, stop

quickly. Right away. Immediately. Two proverbs give us this advice: "He who hurries his footsteps errs" (19:2), and "The heart of the righteous ponders how to answer, but the mouth of the wicked pours out evil things" without thought (15:28).

When you curb these kinds of first responses and reactions and come to a screeching halt, you buy some time—even if it's only seconds—to consider your situation and how to handle it.

Step 2: Wait.

Stopping and waiting can merge together because they flow so naturally into each other. Once you stop before doing anything (or saying anything!), you again buy yourself time to start the process of deciding to do something—and hopefully the right something—or maybe to do nothing.

Waiting before acting or reacting also buys you time to make a real decision.

Waiting gives you the time you need to be a woman of wisdom who "ponders how to answer" and what to say (15:28).

Waiting gives you time to take a deep breath—both in your lungs and in your soul as you utter a prayer to God—so you can respond like the woman in Proverbs 31 did: "She opens her mouth in wisdom, and the teaching of kindness is on her tongue" (verse 26).

Step 3: Search the Scriptures.

In chapter 1 of Proverbs, God tells us, "The fear of the LORD is the beginning of knowledge" (verse 7). That's why we must always look to God first for His wisdom. His Word, the Bible, contains all the wisdom you need and has the answers you need for handling any and every situation. As Ecclesiastes 1:9 states, "There is nothing new under the sun."

After stopping and waiting, we can ask, "What does the Bible say?" Your initial act is to look to God's Word first. Then you can reach out to people who can help support you, pray for you, advise you, and guide you toward God's will.

One blessing of reading your Bible faithfully and regularly is that you begin to know God's principles for managing problems before they happen. Then, when you stop and wait and quickly ask or think, "What does the Bible say about this situation?" you can mentally flip through the pages of the Bible. Amazingly, His answers will likely surface. It's like James 1:5 advises: If you need wisdom, "ask of God, who gives to all generously and without reproach, and it will be given to him."

Step 4: Pray.

After you have searched the Scriptures and reviewed what the Bible says about your situation, speak to God in prayer. When you come before the presence of God in prayer, you can admit to Him your hurt pride, anger, fear, heartache, and other emotions that whirl around you as you work toward His solution. Through prayer you acknowledge God's ability to give you His direction for your decision or response as you follow the advice of these tried and true and—for me—well-loved verses of Proverbs 3:5-6:

> *Trust in the LORD with all your heart*
> *and do not lean on your own understanding.*
> *In all your ways acknowledge Him,*
> *and He will make your paths straight.*

This is what happened to Nehemiah. When Nehemiah was questioned face-to-face by the king and afraid for his life, he prayed to God. Before he uttered a word to the king, Nehemiah took time to shoot a prayer upward. He prayed to the God of heaven—and immediately answered the king (see Nehemiah 2:1-8). Nehemiah prayed on the spot, seeking God's wisdom, and he received it—in seconds! And the pagan king gave Nehemiah everything he asked for to organize God's people to rebuild the wall around Jerusalem.

Like Nehemiah, shoot your on-the-spot "arrow prayers" upward to God, and wait for His answer. He will answer, and He will make your path—your next step or word or decision—straight and clear.

Step 5: Seek counsel.

Proverbs majors on being wise and seeking advice.[1] Seeking counsel is Step 5 for a good reason. For instance, if you make "seeking counsel" Step 2, you can easily react emotionally because you didn't "wait" or "search the Scriptures" or "pray." These omissions can result in seeking the wrong kind of counsel or accepting guidance from the wrong people. Like Rehoboam, you could quickly choose to seek advice from those you know will affirm what you think and what you want to happen.

Think about it: A loved one, or a best friend, or an unbelieving workmate who sees your emotional state might, out of their own emotions, affirm what you want to do, which may not be biblical. When you stop, wait, search the Scriptures, and pray, you are then ready to evaluate the advice others give you with an open heart and a right frame of reference—God's.

And here's some good advice my older mentors passed on to me: If you are married, be sure you run your decision or dilemma by your husband before you talk to anyone else. Find out what he does or does not want you to do. The two of you are one flesh, and he is your "head," your leader, the person who is accountable to God for you. Factor his opinions and desires into this step before you move to Step 6 and make a decision.[2]

Step 6: Make a decision.

After you've taken the first five steps, your decision has a much better chance of being one based on Scripture and wisdom, time, and prayer—not emotion. You can proceed because you have followed the advice of Proverbs 16:3: "Commit your works to the Lord and your plans will be established."

To put your mind at ease, realize this process will sometimes take seconds, minutes, hours, days...or even months. You want to do your best to know what the right thing to do is...before you do anything. You can always ask people for time to pray, time to think this through, time to talk to your husband, time to get some advice. The end result you are searching for is knowing you've done all you can to make a good, solid decision. Your goal is as Romans 14:5 says, "Each person must be fully convinced in his own mind" (Romans 14:5).

Step 7: Act on your decision.

You've done the work. You stopped before you sinned or blundered. You waited patiently and prayerfully. You sought counsel from God through His Word and prayer, then from godly people. You have determined what you believe to be God's leading in dealing with your issue. And now it's time for action.

And be encouraged! You can act with boldness and move forward in confidence, knowing you have consulted God every step of the way. And blessing upon blessings, you can trust Him to give you peace and guide you in His path—or to point you in a different direction. As God promises, when we trust in Him—and not our own understanding—He will direct our path.

As you well know, not a single day goes by that you don't have to make decisions—maybe even a decision per minute! Having a plan means everything when chaos erupts. Working your way through Steps 1–6 is a plan that brings you to Step 7: Act on your decision.

And guess what? You may also need a plan when you launch your decision! For instance, what will you say? How will you act? What will your first step be? Do you need to rehearse?

Like a general marching to war, move out and move forward on your plan. General—and President—Dwight D. Eisenhower ran the U.S. Army and the United States of America with this motto: "Planning is everything!"

God's Wisdom...for Your Day

Our verse for this chapter on getting all the advice you can instructed us to "prepare plans by consultation, and make war by wise guidance" (Proverbs 20:18). You probably put the wisdom from this verse to work every morning as you look at your schedule for the day and then make a to-do list to help you tackle and manage what's coming up. These same acts of preparation (making your lists) and making war (moving forward to tackle your projects) are how we manage our days and our decision making. Our actions are to "prepare" and to "make war," but our preparation includes consulting others—especially God—so our battles are fought only after we obtain guidance.

As you desire to do God's will today, reach heavenward for His wisdom and guidance, come what may! Get all the wisdom you can—from God's Word, from godly people, and through prayer. God will direct your path—and His Word will light your path every step of the way.

21

Planning—and Living— Your Day God's Way

—Life Management—

The plans of the diligent lead surely to advantage,
but everyone who is hasty comes surely to poverty.

PROVERBS 21:5

A Prayer to Pray—

Father of time and all wisdom, I come to You now seeking to set my heart on discovering Your wisdom for my day. As I think on Moses' prayer, "Teach us to number our days," I am reminded of the brevity of my life and the importance of the one singular day that lies before me. With hope in my heart, dear Lord, I am asking You to help me make this day count. May I enter it with an initial plan. May I live it to the hilt! May I bless those You lead across my path. May

I choose to take care of the things that matter most to You and Your purposes, O Father. Guide me with Your wisdom as I attempt to live this one day for You, unto You, and in Your strength and grace. Amen and amen.

I've already shared that I began reading Proverbs daily on the nineteenth day of the month. Well, two days later I crashed into Proverbs 21:5. I was trying to read my proverb for the day early each morning. On this day, I can't remember what happened the night before (a sick child, a loved one I was concerned about, some bills that needed to be paid), but the day I hit Proverbs 21, I was fighting against reading it in a daze of tiredness.

I have to say, the first time I read Proverbs 21:5, it was a wake-up call! If I was a little tired, swoosh...it was gone. My heart went into high gear and my pen came out. Right there in the snow-white margin of my crisp, new Bible, I marked "TM"—a notation that indicated I had found a principle for Time Management. "The plans of the diligent lead surely to advantage."

As I began marking any and all time-management principles in my Bible with TM, my life was turned upside down in a good way. As a new Christian, I began to realize God had a purpose, a direction, and a plan for my life—and I needed a plan to help me team up with His plan.

I was excited and highly motivated about growing as a Christian woman, but I was also terribly frustrated. As I read my Bible each day, I was learning what God wanted for me in my roles as wife, mother, and (gulp) "homemaker," but I didn't know how to start or where to begin. It was like I had a massive elephant in my house, and I didn't know how to get rid of it—or even get around it!

Verse 5 of Proverbs 21 gave me a huge hint about how to tackle the daunting task of growing not only in the Christian faith, but also in managing my responsibilities as a Christian woman. As the joke goes, "Do you know how to eat an elephant?" "No, I don't." "Answer: One bite at a time!" And that's what verse 5 was encouraging me to do. I needed to plan how I was going to tackle and get rid of that very large, very scary elephant. It would have to be one bite—one plan, one action, one day—at a time.

Can you believe it? In only three days of reading Proverbs, I had a plan for my life...or at least my day: I needed to develop some time-management skills! I couldn't do everything to manage my life and my home, but I could plan and I could do *some* things, and hopefully the important things. And it all starts with wise planning. Once again, as the proverb says, "The plans of the diligent lead surely to advantage."

How Proverbs Can Help You Plan for Success

Throughout the Bible, and especially the book of Proverbs, you will see two types of people and women contrasted, which can be seen in everyday life as well. The first group is made up of those who don't plan. They may think they have plans, but in reality what they have are lots of dreams and few, if any, plans. They drift along each day allowing the day to evolve into a plan of its own. They go through their days bouncing from pillar to post, and wonder why they aren't getting anywhere. When they go to bed, they are further behind than when they woke up. They actually moved backward!

Then there is the second kind of person—a wise woman who

is featured in many proverbs, especially the excellent woman of Proverbs 31. I knew right away this was the kind of woman I needed to become: organized, energetic and enthusiastic, active, and productive—and loving every minute of it! And—it's hard to believe—she's actually doing all this without the sound and fury of anger and frustration or the whine of self-pity!

Up to this remarkable day when I discovered the principles in Proverbs 21, I was failing in my home and had developed some bad habits and shortcuts that led to a house that looked more like a pigpen. Suddenly, a little kernel in my heart began to desire to focus my life on following God's will. I realized I wanted to own the responsibility of my roles as a wife and mother and newly appointed "home manager." I began to want to be more like my Master and Savior who did "all things well" (Mark 7:37). I purposed that day to learn how to live out God's plan for me as a woman—to put God first, and take care of my home, make my family a priority.

And, as I read each day, I discovered there was more—much more!—I could learn from Proverbs about planning and living each day God's way, such as:

Planning increases the quality of your life—"The plans of the diligent lead surely to advantage, but everyone who is hasty comes surely to poverty" (Proverbs 21:5). As a new Christian at age 28, I was way behind the curve. I had been married 8 years, had two tiny toddlers, and didn't have a clue about the practical implications of my new life in Christ. I was like a woman on a horse that tried to ride off in all directions at the same time!

Maybe you can sense my frustration, and maybe you get the same feelings at times. But after reading verse 5, I realized it is better to spend a little time making plans than to throw away time on something I haven't thought through. And as I began to plan, I realized the resources that God had given me to work with. I had the support of my fantastic husband (after all, he might get some clean laundry and a nice dinner out of this venture). Plus, I was surrounded by an eager corps of godly women who wanted to help women like me grow as Christian women. And most important of all, I had my Bible—my precious, wonderful Bible!

As I began diligently planning each day with this one principle, I made instant progress and was already experiencing immediate, positive results! As Proverb 21:5 says, "The plans of the diligent lead surely to advantage."

Planning should include God—"The horse is prepared for the day of battle, but victory belongs to the LORD" (Proverbs 21:31). It's important to have plans, so plan like crazy, and make plans galore! But keep in mind that, without God's input, you might end up working against the very will of God. Put God's desires at the center of your planning. Look to Him for wisdom. Seek His heart and direction. Like this proverb says, prepare your battle plan, but make sure you consult God through His Word and prayer so you can participate in His victory. Proverbs 16:3 affirms this same principle: "Commit your works to the LORD and your plans will be established."

Planning involves people—"Prepare plans by consultation, and make war by wise guidance" (Proverbs 20:18). Or, as another translation states, "Don't go ahead with your plans without the advice of others."[1]

As this verse tells us, make your lists of what needs to be done, then create a plan for today. Your next step is to determine which activities and projects on your list are the most important. So be wise: Seek advice and counsel from others. If you are married, what would your husband like to see you accomplish today? What does he think is vital to your family? Who do you know that is an expert in the areas where you need help, advice, or expertise? Create a plan, get advice from others, and then involve the people you need to fulfill your plan. In other words, create your team. And if you have children, always start with, "What can the kids do to help?"

In chapter 20 we met Nehemiah and learned the importance of praying before making decisions. Nehemiah was also a planner. As one man he couldn't do much, but when he planned and involved the people of Jerusalem, they accomplished what others had not been able to do in over 90 years: They rebuilt the wall around the city of Jerusalem in only 52 days! With a solid plan and the advice and approval of others, the people in your life—your family, friends, church members, other women—can become a mighty army.

Planning can keep you from worry—"She is not afraid of the snow for her household, for all her household are clothed with scarlet" (Proverbs 31:21). Life was hard in Bible times. If this someone didn't plan for the winter, this family would be cold and go hungry. You may not be faced with the threat of severe weather or winters or hunger for your family, but the future is filled with uncertainties. You can worry about the future, or you can plan for the future—whether it's how you are going to make next month's rent or car payment, saving for retirement, or putting aside money for your kids' college or braces or uniforms

Planning for tomorrow is time well spent, while worrying about tomorrow is time misspent—and a sin against God, who has promised He "will supply all your needs according to His riches in glory in Christ Jesus" (Philippians 4:19). As another verse says of God, He "is able to do far more abundantly beyond all that we ask or think" (Ephesians 3:20). Worry does not believe God can help, but planning says, with God's help "I can do all things through Him who strengthens me" (Philippians 4:13). Don't let worries about tomorrow keep you from planning and trusting God and enjoying His provision for today... and for all your tomorrows.

Planning is vigilance—"She looks well to the ways of her household, and does not eat the bread of idleness" (Proverbs 31:27). A wise woman is a master planner of all aspects of her life and home life. She is the manager of the home—and her time, and her work. Just thinking about what is at stake should cause every woman to aggressively plan for the smooth running of her life, her time, and her home.

As a vigilant "watch-woman," you are to stand guard, watching carefully over the daily details of your home-sweet-home. This vigilance will help you to fulfill your divine role as overseer of your home—the place where you and your loved ones live. With a heart set on God's kind of beauty and order for your home and some good time-management skills and a plan for each day, by and with God's grace you can manage all that life brings your way.

God's Wisdom...for Your Day

At the beginning of this chapter I made the statement: "I couldn't do everything...but...I could do *some* things." In other words, I needed to learn and practice "planned neglect." Let me explain.

I remember clipping an article out of the *Los Angeles*

Tmes about a concert pianist who was asked about the secret of his success. He answered, "Planned neglect." He then related how he first began to study the piano. He was young, and many things were tempting and tugging on him for his attention and time. So each day he began to take care of those tugging demands. Then, after taking care of all those other things, he would return to his music, meaning his music was getting the leftovers of his time and energy. But one day he made a decision to deliberately neglect everything else until his practice time was completed. That program of "planned neglect" accounted for his success.

It's the same thing for you (and I can definitely say the same for myself!). You can't do everything. Maybe (also like me) you've tried to be all things to all people and ended up failing on most fronts. A solution? Daily develop and fine-tune the strategy of the concert pianist. Plan to neglect nonpriority projects, issues, activities, and distractions in order to complete and manage well those roles and responsibilities that are truly the most important. Then see what you can do with the lesser items on your list.

What are the few areas in your life that are most important in God's eyes? Are you a daughter? Sister? Wife? Mom? If so, these are roles where your planning is most vital. This is your God-given family—a stewardship and priority given to you by God. What one thing can you plan to do today to enrich the lives of those closest to you?

22

Training Up a Child for God
—Parenting—

Train up a child in the way he should go,
even when he is old he will not depart from it.
PROVERBS 22:6

A Prayer to Pray—

My heavenly Father, You are full of grace and truth, and a father to the fatherless. I am humbled to be Your child and able to call You Abba, Father. I come now before Your throne of grace seeking Your guidance and instruction as I raise my children. The desire of my heart is always that they would love You wholeheartedly and follow hard after You. Oh, how I need Your wisdom! Each day is filled with decisions that must be made and should be made by a mom who is filled with Your love, patience, gentleness, kindness, goodness—and self-control. Teach me Your wisdom for shepherding my beloved children. Strengthen me to do what You say. And fill my heart with Your love for my precious ones. Amen.

Getting Off to a Rough Start

When I share my testimony with an audience, I try to paint a picture of Jim's and my early years as a married couple and then as new parents. For the first eight years of our marriage and three years of parenting in the dark, we read and sought help from any and every source. We had no principles, guidelines, or instructions for building our marriage and nurturing a family. We read just about every parenting book that came down the pike and watched TV talk shows ad nauseam, hoping for help from moms, dads, psychologists, educators, and experts—anyone who thought they had something to say about being a parent. We enrolled in community college night classes on marriage and family. And we tried everything we read, only to drift to the next fad that came along.

Getting Real Help

But finally(!), with new life in Christ and our new Bibles and my new goal to read Proverbs every day, I was finding help—real help—and hope for our little family. Three days after I began reading Proverbs on October 19, I encountered the verse of all verses for parents—Proverbs 22:6: "Train up a child in the way he should go, even when he is old he will not depart from it."

I squealed out loud and then immediately marked this verse in my Bible. I also marked it with a "C" in the margin for "childraising." Then I copied it on a three-by-five-inch card and started memorizing it. For the first time in three years of being a parent, I had direction! And better than that, I had God's direction! Needless to say, Proverbs 22:6 became my "mothering verse." My role and job as a mother was clear and concise—"Train up a child in the way he should go."

Getting Down to Raising Children God's Way

The book of Proverbs is a gold mine of help for all mothers! It abounds with God's perfect, 100-percent wise instructions for parents. Here's just a little of what I found that has guided me every day as a mother—and it's all from Proverbs!

Focus on teaching and training your child—Throughout the Bible, and especially in Proverbs 22:6, parents are instructed and expected to faithfully teach and train each child in God's Word and God's ways—"in the way he should go." This is done by steady instruction in the things of the Lord and consistent, loving discipline throughout your child's years in your home. You are to instill in them godly habits—lifelong habits that are explained in great detail in Proverbs. Your role is to teach God's Word to your kids, train them in the way they should go, and pray fervently that, by God's grace, your parenting efforts will be securely embedded in your child's heart and life.

Focus on the direction—"The way of the Lord is a stronghold to the upright, but ruin to the workers of iniquity" (Proverbs 10:29). Here Proverbs tells us as moms that "the way of the Lord" is the way of wisdom and the way of righteousness. These truths provide us with more ammunition—and motivation—for making sure we teach God's Word to our children. They simply must know His ways! So teach your heart out, dear mom! Don't hold back. Be bold. Be vocal. Be consistent and constant. And be praying as you live out your role as a mother after God's own heart.

Focus on the heart—"Watch over your heart with all diligence, for from it flow the springs of life" (Proverbs 4:23). These words were spoken to a youth, and should also be shared often with your children. Jesus amplified this concept in Matthew 12:34 when He said, "The mouth speaks out of that which fills the heart." According to Jesus and Proverbs 4:23, a child's heart attitude directs his or her behavior (and yours too!). Therefore, your instruction and your discipline should address the attitudes of your child's heart. Concentrate on changing your child's heart—their attitude—not on merely changing their outward actions. Rather than being a drill sergeant, you must become a heart surgeon.

Don't avoid discipline—"The rod and reproof give wisdom, but a child who gets his own way brings shame to his mother" (Proverbs 29:15). Yes, as parents we are to discipline and deal with our child's heart. But, as this proverb states, physical discipline is part of the process for training and molding your child's heart toward God's standards. And there are more proverbs that address the practice of faithfully disciplining your children. Don't fail to notice God's reasons and the motivation behind your follow-through on discipline:

- Discipline the child in whom you delight (Proverbs 3:12).
- Discipline diligently the child you love (13:24).
- Discipline while there is hope (19:18).

- Discipline evil out of your child's heart (20:30).
- Discipline a child in the way he should go (22:6).
- Discipline foolishness out of your child's heart (22:15).

Clearly the Bible teaches that to love your child is to discipline your child. This is not an easy concept to grasp, and it's certainly not easy or pleasant to carry it out (at least it wasn't for me). But I found that as I followed God's commands, wonder of wonders, my girls started responding to my direction and instruction. As a parent, you must trust God that what He is asking of you is best for your children and for your parenting. I know from experience that consistent, faithful, loving discipline works.

Live out what you are teaching—"Give me your heart, my son, and let your eyes delight in my ways" (Proverbs 23:26). This is a frightening verse for me as a mom because it means I must model what I am teaching my children...rather than saying, "Do what I say, not what I do." The apostle Paul told other Christians to "be imitators of me, just as I also am of Christ" (1 Corinthians 11:1). Our lives at home lived according to Christ's teachings and example should provide a "coloring book," or a "copybook," for our children to guide them. They will have something they can follow, copy, trace over, use—and trust—as a godly pattern for their lives.

Here is a powerful poem that pictures our children as little copycats. It gives moms a lot to think about!

> A careful [mom] I ought to be,
> a little fellow follows me.
> I do not dare to go astray,
> For fear he'll go the selfsame way.

Not once can I escape his eyes;
Whate'er he sees me do he tries,
Like me he says he's going to be,
That little chap who follows me...

I must remember as I go
Through summer sun and winter snow,
I'm molding for the years to be—
That little chap who follows me.[1]

Enjoy the fruit of your efforts—"Correct your son, and he will give you comfort; he will also delight your soul" (Proverbs 29:17). There's an important principle in this verse: A child who is disciplined and instructed in the ways of God will give you peace and bring delight to your soul.

Generally, children raised in the discipline and instruction of the Lord are more likely to continue on God's path as adults. Although the faith and godliness of your children is ultimately the work of the Holy Spirit, God uses the influence of parents to make a positive impact on their children. A great example of this is Jonathan Edwards, a powerful Puritan preacher from the 1700s.

To document the legacy of Jonathan and Sarah Edwards, A.E. Winship, an American educator and pastor at the turn of the twentieth century, decided to trace out the descendants of Jonathan Edwards almost 150 years after his death. Edwards and his wife had 11 children. Their godly legacy includes: 1 U.S. vice president, 3 U.S. senators, 3 governors, 3 mayors, 13 college presidents, 30 judges, 65 professors, 80 public office holders, 100 lawyers, and 100 missionaries.

At the same time, Winship traced the descendants of a contemporary of Edwards, a man named Max Jukes (or Juke). His research was just as revealing. Jukes's legacy was traced back to 42 different men in the New York prison system. His descendants included: 7 murderers, 60 thieves, 50 women of debauchery, 130 other convicts, 310 paupers (with over 2300 years lived in poorhouses), 400 who were physically wrecked by indulgent living. It was estimated that Max Jukes's descendants cost the state more than $1,250,000 at that time.

This is a powerful example of how a parent's leadership—or lack of it—can have a profound effect on their children.

Parenting is an occupation that is extremely demanding. It requires 24/7 time and attention for about 20 years. But the example of Jonathan Edwards and his wife, Sarah, should encourage you that your efforts are definitely worth it. Whatever you do, don't give up on your parenting. Keep on being the best mother you can be. When you are not seeing the results you desire, that's your opportunity to pray more, to determine to continue to do what God asks of you as a parent—to not give up. That's your opportunity to trust God with the outcome of your faithfulness. Team up with God as you raise the children He has given you.

God's Wisdom...for Your Day

All parents agree and give a hearty "Amen" that parenting is hard. But please, Mom, enjoy your children—today and every day! And again, don't give up! Don't go looking for some place to turn in your mothering badge. Keep falling on your knees and petitioning God for His help and for the hearts of your precious ones. Keep rolling up your mothering sleeves, owning your role as Mom, embracing the work God has given you to do in training up a child for Him. And continue to dive into the thick of parenting each new day.

I can't keep from saying it again: Own your role as a mother. Relish it! God is asking you, along with your child's father—and no one else—to raise your children for Him. He is asking you to give your children your fervent love, your heart, your time, your best, your all, your blood, sweat, and tears...and above all, your prayers—until your final breath taken on earth is expelled.

23

Choosing What You Eat and Drink

—Health—

When you sit down to dine with a ruler,
consider carefully what is before you,
and put a knife to your throat
if you are a man of great appetite.
Do not desire his delicacies,
for it is deceptive food.

PROVERBS 23:1-3

A Prayer to Pray—

O Thou who hears my prayer, I thank You that You indwell me with Your Holy Spirit. Today I especially thank You that the fruit of my union with Your Spirit is self-control. Today may I choose moderation in all things, O Lord. Today and every day You grant me, I desire to eat, drink, and live for Your glory. May I value my body as Your temple and, as such, do only what will bring honor to Your name above all names. Keep my heart tender toward those who hunger and thirst, and help me pursue paths for aiding those who lack and are in need. Amen.

Every woman probably knows this little piece of calorie-saving advice: Don't go shopping for food on an empty stomach. I know it well, and yet several weeks ago, I was pressed for time and dashed into the grocery store on my way home to pick up a few needed items. I had been craving chocolate chip cookies for a while, and I had remained strong in my battle not to think about mixing up a batch from scratch. But when I raced around a food aisle corner and headed for the checkout line, I caught a glimpse of a whole tub of chocolate chip cookie dough, and—would you believe?—one of those tubs ended up in my shopping cart!

Later at home I longingly looked at the directions on the ginormous tub of cookie dough to see how long it would take before I could sink my teeth into a warm cookie. After starting the oven to preheat, I dared to read the part of the label that declared that each cookie was only 120 calories. Whew, that wasn't so bad.

But then I realized (from past experience) that I couldn't eat just one warm cookie, especially if I baked a cookie sheet full of 120-calorie cookies. Then I wondered, if over a span of time I baked all the cookies represented by the dough in that tub, what would be the total damage I would inflict on my body? Here are the stats from the side of the plastic tub, which produced a shriek, "What? That's horrible!" from my lips:

5 pounds of chocolate chip cookie dough per tub
81 cookies per tub
120 calories per cookie
9,720 calories per tub

Better Eating God's Way

God is interested in every single facet of our daily lives. After all, He created us. He loves us. He has saved us and given us eternal life. In fact, He cares so much about us that He even instructs us in His Word about eating habits that maximize our personal health for greater usefulness and ministry to others. When we put God's wisdom and knowledge regarding our health to use, we move toward building a better lifestyle—one that glorifies and honors God as we represent Him to others.

Before we look at a handful of proverbs that guide us in this everyday area of food, consider 1 Corinthians 10:31. This one verse is a spiritual guide to our physical eating and drinking habits. Here the apostle Paul instructs us, "Whether, then, you eat or drink or whatever you do, do all to the glory of God." This is a remarkable truth because as believers we should live and yearn to glorify God. This verse is telling us it is possible for us to glorify and honor the Lord by the way we eat and drink.

A well-known and loved summary statement for believers in Christ reads, "The chief end of man is to glorify God, and to enjoy Him forever."[1] Just think! You can give glory to God in the everyday way you eat and drink. Following a few guidelines found in Proverbs shows you the way to better eating and better living—a way to glorify God.

Rule 1: Restrain yourself, not stuff yourself—"When you sit down to dine with a ruler, consider carefully what is before you; and put a knife to your throat, if you are a man of great appetite" (Proverbs 23:1-2). These verses refer to a test rulers used to determine what kind of person was sitting at their table. Those who overate exposed character flaws of overindulgence and a lack of self-control. Those who were wise, however, ate with moderation and restraint, revealing their inner character traits of wisdom, self-control, respect, and gratitude through this outward action. They were more interested in their host than in their food. They had come to listen and learn and honor their host—not gorge themselves on his food!

Have you ever thought that your eating habits are not only a reflection of your personal inner character, but also of your relationship with God? This proverb says gluttonous, out-of-control eating is so serious that the person who cannot restrain his appetite should figuratively "put a knife" to their throat.

Rule 2: Do not associate with heavy drinkers and gluttons—"Do not be with heavy drinkers of wine, or with gluttonous eaters of meat" (Proverbs 23:20). Drunkenness and gluttony are both seen in the Bible as sin. This alone should be reason enough to avoid such habits and behavior ourselves, and to avoid these types of people as well. But Proverbs 23 goes on to give another reason for avoiding such company: "For the heavy drinker and the glutton will come to poverty, and drowsiness will clothe a man with rags" (verse 21).

Not only do you pay a physical price—drowsiness, laziness, dullness, vomiting—for drinking and eating too much (Proverbs 23:29-35), but you also pay a price financially. Overeating and overdrinking require lots of money. The financial price is often poverty or enormous credit-card debt. I don't think this is how you want to spend your life and your hard-earned cash. But many people do, and they go—as one commentator entitled this passage in Proverbs—"From Revelry to Rags."[2]

Rule 3: Eat only what is sufficient—"Feed me with the food that is my portion, that I not be full and deny You and say, 'Who is the LORD?' or that I not be in want and steal, and profane the name of my God" (Proverbs 30:8-9). I call these verses my "just enough" prayer. They read like a prayer to God, asking Him to feed us with the food that is needful and sufficient for us. Put another way, the person praying is asking God to "give me just enough to satisfy my needs."[3] And why is eating only what is sufficient so important? It's so we don't indulge to the point that we are satiated and forget the Lord, or are tempted to steal food when there isn't enough. It's obvious the extremes of too much or too little affect our character and actions—and worse, our relationship with God.

Rule 4: Eat only what you need—"Have you found honey? Eat only what you need, that you not have it in excess and vomit it" (Proverbs 25:16). Overindulging to the point of vomiting is never pleasant. It also robs us of the very food that is meant to nourish and energize us for health, for taking care of our many responsibilities, and for serving the Lord. God calls us to eat only as much as we need. To keep us from the sin of gluttony, He says we are simply to eat what is enough, to eat to live—not live to eat.

Rule 5: Do not be mastered by anything—"They struck me, but I did not become ill; they beat me, but I did not know it. When shall I awake? I will seek another drink" (Proverbs 23:35). This verse paints a tragic picture of a drunk person. He has become addicted to alcohol to the point that he is beaten by others...and doesn't even feel it, know it, or remember it. Proverbs 23:29-35 is the longest series of verses in the Bible on the subject of the effects of drunkenness. It starts out by asking six questions: "Who has woe? Who has sorrow? Who has contentions? Who has complaining? Who has wounds without cause? Who has redness of eyes?" The answer? "Those who linger long over wine" (verse 30).

Centuries later, the apostle Paul declared, "All things are lawful for me, but I will not be mastered by anything" (1 Corinthians 6:12). "All things" includes both food and alcohol. Paul is saying that because of God's grace he could participate in many things, like eating foods or drinking wine. However, Paul is putting his foot down and personally choosing to refuse to become enslaved or brought under the control or power of "anything" that would harm his testimony and his ministry.

The same is true for you. As a testimony to others and as an act of your will, you can choose to abstain from anything that can master you. In my mind, I think of this concept like being a lion tamer. There I am in the middle of the ring. The lion (my cravings) is perched on a riser with his big paws stretched out to grab me. But I have a big whip in my hand and am cracking it to keep my lion at bay.

God's Wisdom...for Your Day

Today is your brand-new day...which means you will probably eat several times! I once read that the average person has at least 20 food encounters every day...whether that is at a refrigerator, cupboard, fruit bowl on the table, a coffee shop, vending machine, a birthday cake—or an ice-cream shop! On and on our food encounters go.

As you make your way through your glorious new day, the day that the Lord has made and the day that He has given to you, pray. Use the content of Romans 12:1 as your personal heart cry to God: "Lord, today I present my body to you as a living sacrifice, as a spiritual service of my worship. May I live this day in a way that is acceptable to You. Lead me not into temptation." Use God's wisdom from Proverbs guide you each step as you...

> Refuse to be mastered by food or drink
> Refuse to overeat
> Eat with self-control
> Eat just enough
> Eat only what you need

Let's revisit 1 Corinthians 10:31 and make it *Rule 6: Eat in a way that glorifies God*—"Whether, then, you eat or drink or whatever you do, do all to the glory of God." Even the most common acts of eating and drinking can be done in a way that honors our Lord. Imagine it! You can actually eat in a way that brings honor and glory to God! So give God glory and honor Him when you eat, by what you eat, and by how much you eat. And the major side benefit will be thrown in as you follow God's commands—the caliber of your life, as well as your worship, will improve.

> We are unable to glorify God unless our lives are in harmony with him and his precepts. Nothing in our conduct should obstruct God's glory

from being reflected in us. That is, in everything we do and say, no matter how insignificant, the world should be able to see that we are God's people. Exalting God's glory ought to be our chief purpose in this earthly life.[4]

24

Following God's Plan for Success —Diligence—

"A little sleep, a little slumber,
a little folding of the hands to rest,"
then your poverty will come as a robber
and your want like an armed man.
PROVERBS 24:33-34

A Prayer to Pray—

As I bow before You and think about the virtue of diligence, I can't help but recall Your diligence in completing the creation of the world and its inhabitants. Likewise, Your Son came "to do the will of Him who sent Me" and was able to say at His life's end, "It is finished." I desire to take care of the responsibilities You have given me—my loved ones, my home, my work. Help me, dear Lord, to value and watch over my time. Help me today not to be a "Martha," who is obsessed with the busywork of homemaking, but to be a "Mary," who is faithful to sit quietly at Your feet and take care of the better work of worship first—and then move on to diligently get my daily work done "as unto the Lord." Amen.

There is not a week that goes by that I don't receive a request for advice about how to write a book. Usually, the request begins with, "I've always wanted to write a book." Then a question: "What advice can you give me?" And my answer is always the same: "Don't be a wannabe. Write your book." Then I give them some pointers and direct them to some helpful resources.

Every woman—and that includes you—has a powerful story to tell and expert advice and lessons learned to share. You have life-changing information to pass on to others. It's easy to get overwhelmed and give up on your thought of helping others through your experiences. It's easy to find yourself sitting around daydreaming about writing a book or tackling a personal project you're excited about. The harder step is to actually dive in and create an outline, or write a chapter or two, or take those vital initial start-up steps on some other dream.

To write a book one must actually actively attempt to write a book. It's the same with any of your dream projects. Taking action is where the "be's" and "wannabes" are separated. Doing something—doing anything, including writing a book—takes l-o-t-s of time, hard work, and diligence, along with a commitment to stay with your goal until it's finished.

As I think back on my own life, diligence wasn't really my problem as an unbeliever. I can thank my parents for providing two powerful models of a relentless work ethic. In fact, after they retired as schoolteachers, they continued to work with refinishing furniture and buying and selling antiques well into their 90s! No, I had lots of diligence. My problem was direction. I would go off in all directions at once and rarely finish anything—often ending up with nothing to show. But once I became a Christian, I had direction to go with my diligence, thanks to God's grace and His Word!

God's Word showed me His plan and His path for my life as a woman, wife, mom, and a servant in the church. As I continued to read daily in Proverbs, I soon saw that diligence—along with a lack of diligence—is a major theme in not only Proverbs, but throughout the Bible.

God's Plan for Diligence

You may not ever want to write a book, and that's definitely okay! God is always in charge and leads you step-by-step to His plans for your life. But you do have the stewardship of your life and its many responsibilities. Take a look now at some of what you will discover concerning diligence as you read through Proverbs each day.

A lack of diligence leads to poverty—"'A little sleep, a little slumber, a little folding of the hands to rest,' then your poverty will come as a robber" (Proverbs 24:33-34). This proverb illustrates how sloppy, lazy habits can make a person so careless that it leads to neglect, loss, and failure. What begins as just a little slackness—"a little sleep, a little slumber, a little folding of the hands"—progresses to become a way of life. Soon whatever resources we had and could have had are lost just the same as if we were robbed by a bandit (verse 34).

And there's more! These proverbs also speak of diligence and its effect on our life:

> Diligence affects our finances—"Poor is he who works with a negligent hand, but the hand of the diligent makes rich" (Proverbs 10:4).
>
> Diligence affects our livelihood—"He who tills his land will have plenty of bread, but he who pursues worthless things lacks sense" (Proverbs 12:11).
>
> Diligence affects our productivity—"In all labor there is profit, but mere talk leads only to poverty" (Proverbs 14:23).

A lack of diligence lessens our contribution to society—"He also who is slack in his work is brother to him who destroys" (Proverbs 18:9). How many plane crashes, train wrecks, and other tragedies have been traced back to one person who didn't properly do their job? Problems were overlooked—or put on hold for later. Someone just never got around to it! A shortcut was taken. A bolt was left off. A screw was left untightened. But, hey, it was only one bolt, only one screw!

This proverb illustrates how important it is to make an effort to leave things better than we found them, to leave no task we are responsible for undone. To do that extra little thing—like returning the shopping cart to its stall, tidying a room before we leave it, turning off the lights when we leave a hotel room. Diligence is a key way we can contribute positively to society.

Diligence needs to be aimed in the right direction—"Prepare your work outside and make it ready for yourself in the field; afterwards, then, build your house" (Proverbs 24:27). A modern translation of this ancient proverb could read, "First things first!" Because Israel is an agrarian economy, its people have always depended on crops being planted first, before anything else took place, including building a home for the family.

For many people, the message of this proverb could be: "Get a good education before venturing out into the world or before getting married." Or it could mean, "Pay off your bills or student loans before purchasing a home."

For moms this same proverb could mean, "I need to make sure I am diligently nurturing my family, especially the children, before I seek a job outside the home—or before I get heavily involved in ministry, or before I go back to school...or before I tackle writing a book!" For the working mom, it could mean, "I need to make sure all is well with my family before I leave for work—breakfast, lunches to go, kids set for getting to school."

I know these examples don't always work for everyone, but they do give us direction for using our diligence in a priority order and directing our diligence and attention to what's most important. I wrote my first book after both of my daughters married. Writing, like so many other worthy pursuits, is demanding and consuming. And many days it requires early mornings and late nights to meet deadlines. You have your own set of commitments—perhaps preparing your lessons or Bible study notes, or completing your papers or exams as you seek a degree or license.

Wisdom, as the proverb states, prepares its work in a priority order. Wisdom for you and me comes when we ask, "What are the 'first things first' I need to take care of before going on to other less important pursuits?"

Diligence affects our outcomes—"Know well the condition of your flocks, and pay attention to your herds...and there will be goats' milk enough for your food, for the food of your household, and sustenance for your maidens" (Proverbs 27:23-27).

This practical proverb speaks of a landowner's need to diligently keep watch over his herds to make sure they are safe. The result? His committed vigilance would insure that his family always had food. That's the kind of diligence God is asking of you and me as we watch over our "flocks"—our homes and families.

Like a shepherd, you—a shepherdess—are to diligently and passionately "pay attention" and watch over your flock and your home. This includes both the spiritual and physical condition of their hearts and well-being, as well as where they live. Then, as this proverb concludes, with this kind of diligence, yours will be a family and home that enjoys God's provision and blessings.

God's Wisdom...for Your Day

Today—and each day—is a gift of grace from God to you. Wisdom and truths abound in the Bible that are meant to help you with your desire to be more diligent. These scriptures will move and motivate you to live each day for the Lord.

It helps each fresh, new dawn to remember...

...the brevity of life—Many women choose to live their life in a waiting mode, with an "I'll get around to it someday" attitude, or with an "I have all the time in the world" outlook. Everyone is tempted to be lazy. It's the nature of our flesh. However, you have only one life and, as the saying goes, " 'Twill soon be past. Only what's done for Christ will last." Diligence today and every day will help you get your work done and will benefit and bless your family members, your employer, and those who are counting on

your diligence. Diligence will help you achieve a worthy, God-honoring life with fewer and fewer regrets.

...the purpose of life—I have to admit, this is one of the chief catalysts for my desire for diligence. When it sank in that I was made *by* God and *for* God, and that God had a purpose for *me*, I was thrilled! Until that point in my life, I felt like a drifter, unfulfilled, always seeking and searching for something concrete and meaningful. And suddenly, as I realized God had a purpose for me, it was as if a light went on in me or over me, and I became highly motivated. As you think about your life in Christ and His purpose for you and your salvation, it should motivate you to aim at living each day and each minute of the day for the Lord. You'll want each day to count—for the glory of God (Colossians 3:23). The means to fulfilling this purpose is diligence and God's wonderful grace.

...the pace of life—Diligence does not mean maintaining a frantic pace from start to finish. Diligence simply means pursuing a fruitful pace of life from start to finish as you purposefully move through your life on a daily basis. And here's some great news: You can apply diligence to your work at any time with any project. So why not start—or restart—your life of diligence right now? Your goal is, as the Bible says, to let all things be done decently and in order—and to the glory of God!

Dear friend, your diligence should not be seen as a duty but as a delight. Diligence comes from within and reveals your true character. And you can count on it—sometimes you will get a little down or tired. When this happens, lift up your soul and pray. Keep your heart tuned in to God's Word. Rehearse His promises to you. Remember what a mess your life was when you had no direction, no purpose, no love to give to others. Recall the day of your salvation, and rejoice in what God is accomplishing in you as He transforms you into the image of His dear Son. Trust in the Lord with all your heart, and count on His power and grace to assist you to diligently do His will today.

Once you raise your weary head toward heaven, and once you think heavenly thoughts, and once you lift heartfelt praise and thanksgiving to our precious Savior, you will experience renewed strength for your day. For the Lord gives power to the faint, and to those who have no might He increases their strength. You will mount up with wings as an eagle. You will run and not be weary. You will walk and not faint. Like Elijah, God will tend to you, His worn-out child—and you will be able to go on with your day and tend to your responsibilities in the strength of the Lord.[1]

25

Being Faithful in All Things
—Dependability—

Like the cold of snow in the time of harvest
is a faithful messenger to those who send him,
for he refreshes the soul of his masters.

PROVERBS 25:13

A Prayer to Pray—

Dear Searcher of hearts, I thank You that Your mercies are new every morning! Great is Your faithfulness! I bless Your Name today that I can trust You with not only my day but with my life and, more importantly, my soul. Help me to be trustworthy in my service to You and to those You place in my path today. As I depend on You, may I also be a woman others can depend on too. Lord, I yearn most of all to stand before Your Son when my days on earth are done and hear Him say, "Well done, good and faithful servant." Amen.

As a Christian, faithfulness is a mark of God's presence in your life. You manifest God's faithfulness, a fruit of the Spirit, which is on display to all as you walk by the Spirit (Galatians 5:22). This powerful and powerfully important character quality is also a mark of God's wisdom.

Several key scriptures in the Bible strongly encourage all women to be faithful. In the New Testament, we read that women servers and/or female leaders who served in the church were to qualify in four areas: "Women must likewise be dignified, not malicious gossips, but temperate, *faithful in all things*" (1 Timothy 3:11).

Another source of encouragement is found in the Gospels where we witness the extraordinary faithfulness of a group of women who steadfastly ministered to the needs of our Savior. This band of reliable ladies served Jesus physically and supported His ministry financially.

Then the most heroic act of faithfulness from this group of faithful women began as they followed Jesus on His last journey from Galilee to Jerusalem. This trek led these women to the foot of the cross to suffer alongside Jesus through the entire day of His crucifixion and death.

But their journey and faithful friendship and service didn't end with Jesus' death. The fidelity of these loyal ladies still shone bright as they rose early Sunday morning and walked to the tomb where Jesus' body had been placed. They were ready with all that was needed to fully and properly prepare Jesus' body in death—only to see their faithfulness rewarded by being the first people to hear the news of His resurrection![1]

Yet another source of encouragement for being faithful is the book of Proverbs. Prepare yourself for…

Faithfulness on Display

Faithfulness is a refreshing quality—"Like the cold of snow in the time of harvest is a faithful messenger to those who send him, for he refreshes the soul of his masters" (Proverbs 25:13). Imagine how refreshing a cool drink would be to a farm worker—or to you as you work in your garden or take care of your lawn on a hot day. A trustworthy person, worker, or messenger is like an ice-cold drink on a blistering day. This description and image illustrates the benefit, blessing, and ministry a faithful woman has to those she serves and ministers to. She comes through—no matter what.

Faithfulness requires reliability—"Like a bad tooth and an unsteady foot is confidence in a faithless man in time of trouble" (Proverbs 25:19). What happens when you bite down hard with a broken tooth? Ouch! What happens when you put your weight on a broken foot? Another ouch! Your broken tooth and infirm foot will give way and let you down. They are useless, undependable, and a painful bother. You rely on your teeth and your feet to fulfill basic functions like eating, walking, and working.

Now think of those people who depend on you and rely on you for help in time of trouble or when some crucial project is at stake. If you fail to be faithful to do your part, you can be the cause of failure and a disappointment to those who counted on you to come through and do your part.

The same thing happens right under your own roof. Who are the people who live there? If they are family, they are depending on you for meals, for food in the house, for clean laundry, and for general cleanliness and order. What are your responsibilities at church? Whatever they are, prepare early, double-check everything, arrive early, stay late, and see that your part of the ministry is carried out 100 percent to the end.

Faithfulness is required in your speech—"Lying lips are an abomination to the LORD, but those who deal faithfully are His delight" (Proverbs 12:22). Do you want to be a delight to God? Then be faithful in your speech. Be careful about shading the truth, telling white lies and half-truths, and exaggerating beyond what is true. A sure way to bring joy to God and be a delight to Him and to others is to be absolutely honest when you speak. Follow the admonition of Proverbs 14:5 and resolve to always tell the truth: "A trustworthy witness will not lie."

Faithfulness brings healing—"A wicked messenger falls into adversity, but a faithful envoy brings healing" (Proverbs 13:17). In the Bible, Christians are called to be—and referred to as—ambassadors for Christ.[2] We are messengers of the God we serve. The question then becomes, "Are we a good or a poor messenger?" You are the only Bible some people will ever read.[3] Purpose to faithfully live consistently for Christ as a "faithful envoy," as one who blesses others.

Think of the busy, chaotic days everyone encounters. Everyone is suffering—suffering heartbreak, illness, loss, stress, doing without, loneliness. Because of your attention and commitment to faithfulness, you can bring good to others. When you arrive, you bring peace, healing, comfort, success, order, and wisdom to those in need. You are like the doctor who shows up in an emergency room. The people in pain are instantly relieved emotionally and physically. And the healing process officially begins.

The doctor knows what he's doing and knows how to take care of people who are sick and struggling with pain. When you are faithful to take care of your priorities and responsibilities—your family and friendships, your work and your ministry—your very presence means all is well. Let the healing begin!

Faithfulness is essential in your friendships—"Faithful are the wounds of a friend, but deceitful are the kisses of an enemy" (Proverbs 27:6). What is the definition of a friend? It's someone you can trust, someone who's "got your back," someone who will tell it to you like it is. You don't do your friends any favors by being afraid to be honest with them about their actions, attitudes, and decisions. Your role as a loyal friend is to faithfully support their efforts and commitments, and to hold them accountable to God's Word and encourage them to reach for His standards. How they receive that information is up to them. If they are wise, they will accept your criticism as coming from a faithful friend.

Faithfulness brings blessings—"A faithful man will abound with blessings, but he who makes haste to be rich will not go unpunished" (Proverbs 28:20). A faithful man or woman who is honest and does not covet great wealth receives an abundance of blessings. This proverb and others seem to indicate that the person who is a faithful steward of their money will reap financial blessings. By contrast, the person who is obsessed with acquiring wealth quickly, and especially at the expense of other values, will have disastrous consequences. Those who are ambitious and greedy will make mistakes, break laws, lie, and sacrifice their morals. In the end, as the proverb states, they "will not go unpunished." They will suffer disastrous consequences. God asks you to be faithful—not to be ambitious or money hungry. When you are faithful, God promises you "will abound with blessings."

Faithfulness is the finest of gifts—"The heart of her husband trusts in her, and he will have no lack of gain" (Proverbs 31:11). The greatest gift you can bring to your marriage as a wife is trust. The same is true of your friendships. Whether it's the faithful way you deal with money, your children, your home, your family, your friends or workmates, your commitment to faithfulness inspires trust from others. Married or single, trust is the most important ingredient you can offer your family, friends, and those at work. They know they can count on you to keep your word, keep your appointments, and keep being faithful in all areas of your life.

Faithful in the little things. Faithful in the large things. Faithful in all things. These three descriptions perfectly describe Phoebe, a woman we meet in Romans 16:1-2. She is a living example of Jesus' statement that "he who is faithful in a very little thing is faithful also in much" (Luke 16:10). Phoebe was not one of the leaders of any of the churches in and around Corinth. But she was faithful in her vital service to the people where she lived and also in her ministry to the apostle Paul. Because of her trustworthiness, she was given the responsibility of hand-delivering a letter of great significance to the church in Rome—and to you and me today, and to all those who lived in the centuries between.

Can you imagine the Bible without the book of Romans? That was the "letter" this woman hand-carried from Corinth to Rome. If that had been me, I would have been shaking in my sandals! But the ever-faithful, ever-responsible, ever-reliable Phoebe got the assignment—and she got the letter delivered safely into the right hands.

Are you faithful in the little things like giving generously of your time and energy to your church? By helping others, you are providing a great service to God and His people. And who knows, one day God may ask you to provide Him with even greater service! Phoebe was faithful in what was least...and proved faithful also in much.

God's Wisdom...for Your Day

The book of Proverbs gives us a good idea and many word pictures of the nature of faithfulness. But, in reality, what does faithfulness do? What does faithfulness in action look like? I have asked this question of myself for many years as I've studied the Bible and read through Proverbs. Here is an inventory I put in my book *A Woman's Walk with God.*[4]

Hopefully these points will stretch your understanding about the quality of faithfulness. It's a desperately needed trait in our world today. If you were to follow a woman who is walking with God by His Spirit, you would observe these acts of faithfulness in her daily life:

- She follows through—on whatever she has to do.
- She comes through—no matter what.
- She delivers the goods—whether a message or a meal.
- She shows up—even early so others won't worry.
- She keeps her word—her yes means yes and her no means no (James 5:12).
- She keeps her commitments and appointments—you won't find her canceling without a solid reason.

- She successfully transacts business—carrying out any instructions given to her.

- She discharges her official duties in the church—and does not neglect worship.

- She is devoted to duty—just as Jesus was when He came to do His Father's will (John 4:34).

You can use this as a checklist—or a prayer list—for yourself. Ask God to point out any areas where you need improvement or need to be more faithful. Ask Him for His strength to go to work on cultivating His faithfulness in your daily life.

26

Getting Rid of Laziness —Personal Discipline—

The sluggard says, "There is a lion in the road!
A lion is in the open square!"
As the door turns on its hinges,
so does the sluggard on his bed.
The sluggard buries his hand in the dish;
he is weary of bringing it to his mouth again.

PROVERBS 26:13-15

A Prayer to Pray—

O Divine Redeemer, You have transformed not only my heart, but also my will and emotions. Give me the resolve this day to discipline my body, to make it my slave, and to do the work You've called me to. My heart's desire is to effectively serve You and those in my family and any others You bring across my path today. May Your Holy Spirit empower me to deal with any laziness and selfishness that would keep me this day from being an instrument worthy to be used in my Master's service. Amen.

Whether we like it or not, we live in an "instant gratification society." We want everything…and we want it now, preferably with as little effort as possible! Whether it's entertainment, starting a small business, learning a new skill or language, or losing weight, it doesn't matter. If results can't be achieved quickly in a few hours or days, we promptly give it up and slide back into our old, familiar routines that offer some gratification while requiring little or no effort on our part.

Bible study is a terrific example. Most, if not all, Christians agree that reading and studying the Bible is important. Think about it: The Bible contains God's Word and His will. God has communicated it to us in one book, written by God Himself! It's a miracle! And it contains vital information for every facet of life—"everything pertaining to life and godliness" (2 Peter 1:3). Tragically, many Christians simply don't make the effort. It's too easy to be lazy in the mornings. And it's quite natural (and also easy) to live out what Proverbs 26:14 states—"As the door turns on its hinges, so does the sluggard on his bed."

The #1 reason why people don't read their Bible just might be we are lazy. We would rather turn over in bed and snooze for another 10 minutes…and another 10 minutes…and another… than make even a tiny effort to get out of bed, slap a pod into the instant coffeemaker, press "brew," and locate our Bible.

How can women like you and me overcome the lethargy and laziness that can keep us from reading God's Word? From growing spiritually?

A Surprise Answer

Several months after Jim and I started out on our spiritual journey as new Christians, we attended a Bible seminar sponsored by our first-ever church. The man speaking was a professor and author and chief editor for a top Christian magazine. He had done much in his early days to defend the Christian faith against liberal thinking. It was evident throughout the one-day seminar that he really knew his Bible!

At the end of the event, Jim wanted to meet this man and try to find out his "secret" about how he came to know the Bible so well. And, of course, Jim wanted me to go with him. We expected this knowledgeable man to say it was his solid Christian upbringing from the cradle up to adulthood. Or maybe it was his theological training at an outstanding seminary. Or maybe it was his hard-earned expertise and ability to translate and interpret Scripture.

The answer was no to all of the above. To our surprise, he answered, "Whatever I know or have accomplished is the result of a lifetime of regularly and systematically reading through the Bible. That discipline has given me a depth of understanding God's Word."

Pretty simple, right? Jim and I just stood there, both thinking at the same time, "I need to get a solid grasp on God's Word, so I better get started today on my own 'lifetime' of reading through the Bible!"

Discipline: Don't Start Your Day Without It!

Dear sister, that seminar lasted for only one day, but that bit of advice from the humble speaker has had a lifelong impact on my husband and me. I still attempt on a daily basis to read my Bible. And, as I've shared throughout this book, this routine has included reading through the book of Proverbs day by day, which has led me to today's date—Day 26 of the current month. And it just happens to be the day I am writing on Proverbs, chapter 26! And, oh dear. There it is again, in all its glory—the subject of discipline and the lack of discipline, also known as laziness. Ouch!

God has a few nuggets of divine wisdom for us about discipline versus laziness.

Discipline does not make excuses—The lazy sluggard says, "There is a lion in the road! A lion is in the open square!" (Proverbs 26:13). This person is worried about two kinds of lions: one "in the road" and the other "in the open square." Yet, both appear to be far-fetched excuses to explain why this lazy person is not going to leave his house to go to work. In Proverbs 22:13, another lazy sluggard excused himself from work saying, "There is a lion outside; I will be killed in the streets!"

It's amazing how you and I can think up ten different reasons for not doing a load of laundry...or making the bed...or for postponing cleaning or getting groceries. When we make excuses and create reasons why we cannot do our work, our excuses keep us from following God's instructions to us to be "workers at home" (Titus 2:5), to do as God's excellent woman does who "looks well to the ways of her household, and does not eat the bread of idleness" (Proverbs 31:27).

Discipline fuels ambition—"As the door turns on its hinges, so does the sluggard on his bed" (Proverbs 26:14). This verse likens the sluggard's movements in bed to a door swinging back and forth on its hinges. He looks like he might be getting up to do something productive...but then he falls back on his pillow. Self-discipline does the opposite. It gives you the drive to get out of bed in the morning and meet the day, to tackle your projects and your work—to make sure you have time with the Lord.

Each new day is a day God has made, and you should want to live it to the hilt, to its fullest! You have a day filled with goals to be achieved, people to care for, and a home to manage. And amazingly, not one of these responsibilities will be accomplished until you get out of bed!

Discipline overcomes laziness and generates energy—"The sluggard buries his hand in the dish; he is weary of bringing it to his mouth again" (Proverbs 26:15). You almost have to laugh as you read this proverb! It describes the person who conforms to a simplified version of Newton's First Law of Motion which states, "An object at rest tends to remain at rest." This opposing law is also true: "An object in motion tends to remain in motion." The lazy sluggard's inertia keeps that person from generating enough energy to move forward and be productive. Discipline gets you moving...and keeps you moving, even when you're tired.

Discipline keeps you growing—"The sluggard is wiser in his own eyes than seven men who can give a discreet answer" (Proverbs 26:16). The lazy person has spent his life justifying (at least in his own mind) why he doesn't need to exert himself. Whenever advice is given to him for overcoming his problem of laziness, the indolent person has a long list of superior reasons why no suggestion or admonition will work. This includes the wisdom of "seven men," who could have helped him be more productive.

Please don't be a woman, who, like the sluggard in the Bible, is lazy and has stopped growing! It happened the second she became satisfied with her life—and no one was going to change her. For this woman, laziness is a dead end. There will be fewer and lesser accomplishments, productivity, goals, ambitions, dreams-come-true. She has accepted that what she is doing and not doing is the right thing for her. She is no longer looking for any help, answers, or change—or growth. Why would she seek help or want to change when doing so would require effort?

By contrast, the woman who is wise is disciplined. She's in a one-woman war against laziness. "She rises also while it is still night," and "Her lamp does not go out at night." She "does not eat the bread of idleness." She is not afraid of work. In fact, "She girds herself with strength and makes her arms strong." This woman is always looking for any aid or information she can find that will help her do her work better—and faster.[1]

God's Wisdom...for Your Day

Your journey toward greater discipline begins with the single first step of desire. And the strongest desire of all is love. When you love the Lord, you long to serve the Lord—and that requires discipline and action. Likewise, when you love others your heart desires to serve and assist them, to better their lives, which requires discipline and action. And when you follow the Lord's commandment to "love your neighbor as yourself," you will want to serve God's people, your neighbors, and your acquaintances—and that also requires discipline and action.

Proverbs 31 speaks of the excellent woman as blessing all those whose lives she touched. This short list of her love, her labors, and her personal discipline is God's checklist for you too—all found in Proverbs 31:10-31:

She does her husband good and not evil all the days of her life.

She works with her hands in delight.

She brings her food from afar.

She gives food to her household.

She plants a vineyard.

She stretches out her hands to the distaff and her hands grasp the spindle.

She extends her hands to the poor and needy.

She makes coverings for herself and her family.

She makes linen garments and sells them.

What, we wonder, was her motivation? Again, it is love—an all-consuming love for the Lord: She is "a woman who fears the LORD" (verse 30). Her heart and soul of love fueled and empowered her work, her labors of love.

After enumerating her virtues and efforts, God made this crowning statement regarding the noble woman of Proverbs 31: "Let her works praise her in the gates" (verse 31). As renowned preacher G. Campbell Morgan commented, "The woman celebrated in Proverbs 31 is the one who realizes in all fullness and richness the capacities and glories of her womanhood."

Yes, personal discipline is required for all your endeavors and for all your successes in the many roles and responsibilities God has assigned to you. You've probably had this experience after a long, trying, packed, and filled-to-the-brim day. As you—at last!—are able to climb into your bed-sweet-bed, it just seems natural to think back through the day and your to-do list with all the dreams you had of all the progress you would make. It's so easy at this moment to tilt to the conclusion that "the glass is truly half empty." That your day wasn't successful. That your list for tomorrow will be even longer as you carry over the work that didn't get done today. As you set your focus on all that you didn't get done, your overwhelmed spirit matches your spent body at your day's end.

But gloriously, magnificently, and triumphantly, a new day arrives. Its dawning is accompanied by light and a newness of life. The air is clean, fresh, and cool. The world is quiet or slowly approaching its start-up mode. No words better describe the blessed arrival of a fresh, new day than these in Lamentations 3:22-24:

> *The LORD's lovingkindnesses indeed never cease,*
> *for His compassions never fail.*
> *They are new every morning;*
> *great is Your faithfulness.*
> *"The LORD is my portion," says my soul,*
> *"Therefore I have hope in Him."*

Just for today—for your brand-new day—faithfully set out once again. Look to the Lord in hope. Give thanks to Him for His faithfulness. Pray to follow in His steps. Then begin again to bless others through your personal discipline, through what you do accomplish. Set your sights on the present, on today. After all, as the saying goes, "What you are tomorrow, you are becoming today."

27

Being Careful in a Careless World

—Common Sense—

A prudent man sees evil and hides himself,
the naive proceed and pay the penalty.
PROVERBS 27:12

A Prayer to Pray—

O Father, how I long for the quality of common sense to mark me as a woman after Your own heart! You are the God of all wisdom, and in Proverbs You give Your people a massive amount of wisdom—Your wisdom for the days and challenges of our lives. All of Your instructions are perfect. All of Your actions are utterly holy, righteous, and bear the mark of wisdom. Today I am crying out for Your wisdom. My days are hectic and packed full. So many important decisions come my way—decisions that make a difference. May

Your Spirit guide me today to carefully make right choices as I encounter a variety of people and problems—to make Your choices. Amen, and thank You!

When I became a Christian, my emotions, attitudes, and social biases were already set in stone…or so I thought. But praise God, Jesus Christ changed all that! I was "a new creature" in Christ (2 Corinthians 5:17)—a newborn baby believer—and I knew it. Twenty-eight years of doing things my way had only gotten me to the end of my rope, so to speak. But the book of Proverbs came to my rescue.

As I began reading Proverbs each day, I encountered verses like this one: "The way of a fool is right in his own eyes, but a wise man is he who listens to counsel" (Proverbs 12:15). My response? "Oh my! I'm that fool!" That very day I started looking for help, for books, for a Bible study to join, for mentors who could give me direction for my new life in Christ. "The old things" were passed away (2 Corinthians 5:17), and, thanks be to God, that included most of my worldly views and ways.

The heart is the seat of our emotions and attitudes, and God went to work on mine. He began to change my heart…which affected my actions and reactions in the areas of daily discretion in practical life, also known as "common sense."

Wisdom for Daily Life

Proverbs 27 is packed with verses that show us how practical wisdom, or prudence, is needed for everyday, down-to-earth living. Verse 12 describes the actions of a prudent person. Even if you don't care for the old-fashioned word "prudent," you'll like its meaning—and you'll definitely benefit from having it!

Simply stated, prudent means being careful or restrained in your actions and decision-making.

The person who possesses the quality of prudence is described as one who is wise, sensible in practical affairs, discreet, sober, and careful. One commentator defines prudence as seen here in Proverbs 27:12: "Prudent men are cautious and pull back from danger while foolish men who are oblivious to risk keep going. They will eventually suffer for their carelessness."[1]

As you can see, prudence is a must-have quality in your daily life as a busy woman who carries a heavy load of responsibilities. Much of each day we must make a decision a minute. Prudence definitely improves the quality of those decisions.

And even more important and more motivating is knowing that prudence is a quality that is highly valued by God. In fact, the New Testament states that an "elder" or "overseer" or leader in the church must exhibit this quality: "An overseer...must be... prudent..." (1 Timothy 3:2).

Here is a handful of verses in Proverbs that will help us with everyday life:

Prudence is perceptive—"A prudent man sees evil and hides himself, the naive proceed and pay the penalty" (Proverbs 27:12). When you use your spiritual eyes (which are developed by reading and studying your Bible), you are able to "see" what's happening around you. It's like you've sprouted antennae or radar for spotting trouble ahead.

Once you can see what's happening, prudence can guide your response. If what's occurring is questionable or frightening or evil, this scripture tells you the right and wise thing to do. It's as if wisdom is shouting, "Don't just blindly keep moving forward. That's what the naive do. They don't see or sense or think about the danger. Therefore, they will suffer the consequences. You must be prudent and run, leave, move! Hide yourself!"

We could also say that a prudent woman walks warily. To be a prudent woman, form the habit of fully evaluating your actions before you make a move. Always ask, "Does this activity or decision go against Scripture?" If it does, participating in that activity is out. Doing so would be classified as choosing to go against God's revealed will, as being "evil." Therefore, this choice is not an option. Your actions and responses are clear: Say no. Leave the scene. Turn around and go the other way. Flee from the situation.

Every married woman learns sooner or later that it takes two to fight as a couple. It's sort of like a boxing match—only it occurs in your home, your living room, or your car. There are two fighters in the ring: your husband wearing blue trunks over in his corner, and you in pink shorts in the opposite corner. When the bell rings, two fighters are expected to come out and fight until one is beaten or knocked out or gives up or loses.

But what happens if, when the bell rings, only one fighter comes out? It's obvious: There is no fight. There can be no fight. Why? Because it takes two to have a fight.

I learned in my marriage to try my best not to initiate an argument—and not to participate in an argument. I learned to do the same thing at church, or when talking to a neighbor: When a situation or opposing view gets hot, I was to do what this proverb says and excuse myself.

When a discussion gets hostile or uncomfortable or out of control, you always have the right to ask to think about whatever the issue is, to pray about it, to search the Scriptures about it, and to seek counsel about it. And, if you are married, you have the right—and the responsibility—to talk it over with your husband.

This principle of prudence from Proverbs 27:12 is often used to help women whose husbands are prone to anger, violence, physical assault, or alcohol or drug addiction. When a situation gets heated and is moving toward an argument or outburst, the woman involved can "hide" herself by leaving the room, going to another room, going upstairs or downstairs, going outside. As another proverb states, "A gracious woman retains honor" (Proverbs 11:16 NKJV). You obtain and retain honor and win respect by staying away from and out of quarrels, arguments, and fighting. God will give you all the grace you need to be gracious and respond with His grace and graciousness.

Prudence exercises self-control—"A fool's anger [vexation] is known at once, but a prudent man conceals dishonor" (Proverbs 12:16). It doesn't take long for a foolish woman to explode. She can blow up at the slightest aggravation. It's become a way of life. But the prudent woman knows how to ignore an insult and to exercise self-control.

In the beautiful devotional book *The One Year Book of Proverbs*, I found these thoughts and instructions:

> A wise person realizes that an insult says more about the insulter than the insulted. He or she takes a deep breath and takes the long view. Staying calm, in this case, becomes not a passive, wimpy reaction but an active response drawn from inner strength and assurance that what the other person thinks or says is not the final word. We take our cue from God himself...[who was] "slow to anger."[2]

This author then quotes James 1:19-20: "My dear brothers and sisters, be quick to listen, slow to speak, and slow to get angry. Your anger can never make things right in God's sight" (NLT).

Jesus is our perfect example of one who ignored the insults of others throughout His life, during His trial, and while in agony on the cross. Pilate saw something different in Jesus' lack of response or retaliation and "was amazed" (Mark 15:5). This humble, Christlike behavior is what God wants from you and me when someone insults or slanders us.

Prudence is modest—"A prudent man conceals knowledge, but the heart of fools proclaims folly" (Proverbs12:23). A true lady doesn't go around showing off how much she knows, or spouting off her credentials or past accomplishments. She discreetly conceals her learning. It's not that she doesn't use her knowledge and draw on God's multiple blessings in her life, but she doesn't use it to impress.

Summed up, God's lesson in wisdom is: Talk less. Keep the spotlight off yourself. Focus on others. Minister to them. Learn from them. Don't be a "Here I am!" woman. Be a "There you are!" woman.

Prudence reveals character—"Every prudent man acts with knowledge, but a fool displays folly" (Proverbs 13:16). In Hebrew thinking, "knowledge" was what made up the totality of a person—their heart, soul, and mind. To a Hebrew, knowledge was both will and emotions. In a word, it was character. A woman's conduct, therefore, reveals her character. If a woman is prudent, it is revealed in the responsible way she lives her life, while a foolish woman's conduct reveals her folly.

Just think of what having knowledge or prudence can do for you! In your daily life, it guards you against unforeseen dangers and helps you find ways to escape or avoid trying situations and difficulties. Prudence is essential for training your children, for directing your family affairs, and for caring for your household responsibilities. Prudence is important! To make a big difference in the way you handle life and the people in it, each day ask God for a fresh dose of prudence for your fresh, new day... before you get out of bed!

Prudence says very little—"He who restrains his words has knowledge, and he who has a cool spirit is a man of understanding. Even a fool, when he keeps silent, is considered wise; when he closes his lips, he is considered prudent" (Proverbs 17:27-28). These two proverbs could be entitled "Think Before You Speak." A wise person stays cool and keeps their mouth shut. In fact, such self-control is viewed as wisdom, even if it is practiced by a fool (verse 28). To be thought of or known as a wise or prudent woman, all you have to do is close your lips and keep them shut. The first step toward wisdom and prudence is to close your mouth.

Prudence is a choice—"House and wealth are an inheritance from fathers, but a prudent wife is from the LORD" (Proverbs 19:14). It's interesting to note that verse 13 which precedes this proverb spoke of the "contentions of a wife." Together these verses show us two kinds of wives—those who help, and those who hurt. This prompts married women to ask, "Am I choosing to complain and nag, or am I choosing to build up and encourage my husband? Am I choosing to be a prudent wife?"

Remember Abigail from chapter 8? She was a prudent wife in spite of her awful husband. He was something else! Yet, regardless of her husband's foolish, obnoxious behavior, Abigail exhibited many of the characteristics of prudence we have studied in this chapter. Her life (see 1 Samuel 25:1-43) provides a great model of a prudent woman and wife and creates a checklist for you:

- She was perceptive of the needs and moods of the moment.
- She exercised self-control by saving the day rather than lashing out.
- She was modest and humble as she fell on the ground to appeal before King David.
- She revealed character by her every action, words spoken and not spoken, and quick thinking that led her to a positive solution to a life-threatening situation.
- She had little to say other than to beg for the lives of her people, appease an angry king, and appeal to her drunken husband.
- She revealed the wisdom she had learned from living with a proud and angry bully.

God's Wisdom...for Your Day

Wherever God finds you today in this world, whether in a job, or at home, or both, don't lose sight of this amazing quality of prudence. It is valued by God, as you have seen in Proverbs. Such common sense will be a faithful companion as you walk through your day—and your life. And, as Proverbs 19:14 reminds us, if you are married, your prudence is a gift from the Lord to your husband.

28

Cultivating a Generous Heart —Finances—

He who gives to the poor will never want,
but he who shuts his eyes will have many curses.
PROVERBS 28:27

A Prayer to Pray—

Keep me neutral, Father! Give me neither poverty nor riches. Feed me with the food that is my portion. Give me just enough! Keep my eyes heavenward, with my gaze intent upon laying up treasure in heaven. Help me not to worry when I think there's not enough, or my stability is rocked and my trust in You is tested. Help me to hold what I do have lightly—not tightly, to be generous to others, responsible with our debts, and ever thankful for what I do have. Melt my heart for others and for Your worldwide causes. Amen from Your grateful child!

Money is an everyday factor of life. And it comes with a set of problems. As an unknown observer dryly concluded,

> You can't win! If you run after money, you're materialistic. If you don't get it, you're a loser. If you get it and keep it, you're a miser. If you don't try to get it, you lack ambition. If you get it and spend it, you're a spendthrift. If you still have it after a lifetime of work, you're a fool who never got any fun out of life.[1]

Yes, money is an everyday factor of life. It's also the source of great pleasure...and the instigator of ulcers, ill health, and wrecked relationships. Money can be used for great good...and for great evil. We are so fortunate that our all-wise God placed a primer on money and finances right in the middle of the Bible in the ever-practical, always-helpful book of Proverbs.

You are not alone in your struggle with money and money management. Government leaders, businesses, families, and even churches get trapped into thinking money is the answer to every problem. As a result, it's easy to think having more money will solve all our problems.

Money is dangerous if we think it's the easiest and only way to get what we want. But with the practical need for money also comes a warning in the Bible about a wrong attitude toward money: "The love of money is a root of all sorts of evil" (1 Timothy 6:10). When money becomes our idol, it comes between us and our relationship with God.

A Budget Without God

When we became a Christian family, Jim and I and our two girls were a typical little pagan family. We spent every penny we earned and used every credit card we had to the max. We even dipped into a loan or two against our mortgage in order to have the lifestyle we desired—a lifestyle which included a nice home, cars, motorcycles, campers, and vacations galore! So when we started attending church and began to understand stewardship and giving or tithing, we discovered that, in our lifestyle budget, nothing was left for God.

At first, our thinking went something like this: *Well, obviously God has gotten along without our money up until now, so He shouldn't mind if we go to church, worship Him, celebrate our salvation...and move right along without including giving to our church and its ministries in our budget.*

Oh, we were soooo wrong! As we read our Bibles and observed the examples of other believers, we realized we needed to have a better understanding of money and finances from God's perspective. The book of Proverbs is loaded with practical wisdom about our attitudes toward money and how to use money. Here are a few things we can learn from Proverbs 28 about this major everyday topic of money.

Handling money is a learned art—"A faithful man will abound with blessings, but he who makes haste to be rich will not go unpunished" (Proverbs 28:20). You've probably heard the expression, "Be careful what you wish for." That's what this proverb is saying. Proverbs warns again and again against wealth gained unscrupulously, too quickly, and at the expense of others.[2]

Learning how to handle money is an art that comes from prayerfully and faithfully taking care of your finances each and every day. It involves hard work to earn the money, and calls for long-range planning and saving for your family and for hard times ahead. It is learned through long, diligent, disciplined, repetitive oversight, and through practice and experience.

This person—the faithful, diligent, and careful man in verse 20—"will abound with blessings." Those who are in a hurry to get rich will be tempted to fudge, cheat, lie, gamble, break the law, and disobey God's Word. They will quickly fail and "will not go unpunished."

Having money does not create happiness—"A man with an evil eye hastens after wealth and does not know that want will come upon him" (Proverbs 28:22). Those who have a grasping spirit, selfish motives, and "an evil eye" spend their brainpower, time, and energy rushing after money, only to find spiritual poverty on the other end of their quest.

Read the proverb again. It's saying that having money does not change your heart or promise happiness. No one has ever met a happy miser. A selfish, greedy heart does not change or go away just because you become rich. It will remain just as cold and empty as it was without the wealth! In the words of an anonymous thinker, "Money is an article which may be used as a universal passport to everywhere except heaven, and as a universal provider of everything except happiness."[3]

Trying to obtain money is the wrong path to take—"A greedy man stirs up strife, but the one who trusts in the LORD will be enriched" (Proverbs 28:25 ESV). The grasping or greedy seeker of money is prone to push everyone and everything else aside in their race for riches and power. Their lack of concern for others leads to great strife and heartache, especially in their relationships. It's true that "the love of money can lead to relational ruin. But wise management of money—and a heart that's focused on God—can make a positive difference in your life and the lives of those you love."[4]

Those who desire to do God's will and who trust Him to

provide will enjoy peace and satisfaction. Jesus said it perfectly, of course: "Seek first His kingdom and His righteousness, and all these things shall be added to you" (Matthew 6:33)—"things" like food, water, and clothing—everything you need to stay alive.

Sharing your money can be a tool for helping others—"He who gives to the poor will never want, but he who shuts his eyes will have many curses" (Proverbs 28:27). This is a recurring theme throughout Proverbs: "The generous man will be prosperous, and he who waters will himself be watered," and "He who is generous will be blessed, for he gives some of his food to the poor" (11:25; 22:9).

These proverbs tell us those with a generous spirit toward people in need will not go unrewarded, but those with a selfish spirit "will have many curses." The Bible doesn't say what those curses might be, but the message is loud and clear: Don't go down that road—the road of selfishness and stinginess. Remember the poor! Open your eyes, your heart, and your wallet to those in need. Share from that which God has given you. When you do, as the three proverbs above promise, you "will never want," you "will be prosperous," and you "will be blessed."

Your generosity doesn't have to be limited to money only. Maybe your money is in tight supply right now, but you can give in other ways, like your time, your help, your talents. The Proverbs 31 woman was praised for giving physical care: "She extends her hand to the poor, and she stretches out her hands to the needy" (verse 20).

You may not have a lot of money, but you have so much that you can give! Jesus' disciples didn't have much money, but as they traveled with their Lord to spread the gospel, they helped, fed, and served those in need in small ways. When your heart is fixed on God and desires to obey His will and follow Jesus' example, the selfishness you harbor will dissipate and the unselfish use of your possessions will emerge. As Jesus, the giver of all—even His life—teaches us, "Do not store up for yourselves treasures on earth...but store up for yourselves treasures in heaven...for where your treasure is, there your heart will be also" (Matthew 6:19-21). Your obedience to Jesus' commands will make you the possessor of spiritual prosperity far beyond any personal sacrifice!

Giving money is a way to honor God—"Honor the Lord from your wealth and from the first of all your produce; so your barns will be filled with plenty and your vats will overflow with new wine" (Proverbs 3:9-10). The Jews of the Old Testament were encouraged to follow the commands of Scripture and give God the "first fruits" of their harvest. As a result of their faith and obedience, God promised bulging barns and overflowing vats of wine. The way you use your money is a test of your trust in God and your relationship with Him.

Do you give to God "off the top"? Do you give Him the best? Or do you give Him some of whatever is left over at the bottom of your paycheck? That's the challenge this proverb extends to you. You honor God when you put Him first, whether it's with your money, your service, your time, or your skills. God is not honored when He is an afterthought in your life.

God's Wisdom...for Your Day

Most people and families—and maybe you too—are simply trying to stay afloat financially. That makes it hard at times to think about giving some of your hard-earned money to your church and to others. But this kind of thinking is an error. You must realize you are not giving to others or even to a church. You are giving to God as an act of worship.

When it comes to your giving, the issue is not how much you give, but your heart attitude when you give. This is a part of what brings about God's blessings upon you. As Proverbs 11:25 states, "The generous man will be prosperous, and he who waters will himself be watered."

Dear friend, there is nothing more beautiful than a gracious, caring, bountiful, giving woman. As you fill your soul each day with God's Word, your heart will overflow in a multitude of good works. Only it won't be work! And it won't be because you have to. And it won't be to get something back in return. No, giving from your heart will be pure joy, motivated by pure love for God, who has given so much to you. It will be passed on from you to others from your pure heart.

Think of our gracious, giving Lord. When He moved among the people, He gave to them, reached out to them, taught them, helped them, fed them, healed them, and ministered to them. Imagine the hope in the heart of the woman who had suffered for 12 years from a physical ailment and thought, "If only I may touch His garment, I shall be made well" (Matthew 9:21 NKJV)...and then stooped to do so. Our Jesus delighted in healing her!

Think, too, about the frantic father who begged Jesus to save his young, dying daughter, and our Savior—moved with compassion and full of mercy—reached out His hand and raised her from the dead.

And think about the multitudes who were hungry and needed food, and Jesus gave it to them—so generously, abundantly, and bountifully that there were leftovers!

My friend, you simply cannot outgive God. So give! And when you do, give gloriously, freely, lovingly, and with prayer! God will honor your generous heart. You will be blessed and be a blessing to others.

This proverb is a God-given prayer that will safeguard your heart against greed today and every today:

Give me neither poverty nor riches;
feed me with the food that is my portion.
(Proverbs 30:8)

29

Humbling Yourself Before God —Humility—

A man's pride will bring him low,
but a humble spirit will obtain honor.
PROVERBS 29:23

A Prayer to Pray—

Father God, today I am asking Your help in growing a heart that desires humility, a heart that delights in time spent on my knees in worship, adoration, and prayer. I want to walk humbly with my God, to humble myself beneath the mighty hand of God, trusting You to exalt me in due time. Mold me into a woman who loves and humbly serves others, a woman who bows regularly to pray for others, a woman who carries the example of Your Son's and my Savior's humble nature in my heart. Amen.

God is faithful to teach us about our human emotions, and aren't you glad? They can sure sneak up on us and freak us out...or land us in full-blown depression. But our faithful Lord tells us in His Word how to manage them His way.

As with many other emotions, the topics of pride and humility are boldly and often addressed in the book of Proverbs. I heard a preacher share this joke in a sermon: "I could relate some of my many instances where I displayed great humility, but alas, once I did that, I would only have revealed my pride!" So, as we turn now to the virtue and character quality of humility, let me pass on another story:

> Professor Smith was climbing the Weisshorn. When near the top, the guide stood aside to permit the traveler to have the honor of first reaching the top. Exhilarated by the view, forgetful of the fierce gale that was blowing, he sprang up and stood erect on the summit. The guide pulled him down, exclaiming, "On your knees, sir; you are not safe there except on your knees."[1]

This story reminds us that no one is safe from pride. Any success we enjoy, whether it's climbing mountains, getting a good education, writing books, or any other area of accomplishment, pride is a very real possibility and a serious threat. Therefore, with each measure of success you and I experience, the only protection from pride is to be constantly "on your knees." Proverbs has much to teach us about the battle between pride and humility and how to live on our knees in our hearts and minds.

The Number One Enemy of Humility Is Pride

Pride is a heart issue—"Haughty eyes and a proud heart, the lamp of the wicked, is sin" (Proverbs 21:4). Pride is basically an attitude of the heart and spirit, and when pride begins to grow in a person's heart (which is the seat of their character), destruction is not far behind! Note the progression of sinful behavior leading to destruction:

- First, a man's heart is haughty. Pride can assume an arrogance that is described as "haughty eyes." As with so many sins of attitude, pride cannot remain internalized. It even shows up in the eyes! As Proverbs 18:12 warns, "Before destruction the heart of man is haughty."

- Next, what is in the heart will soon surface and infect a person's speech, leading that person to boast. Jesus noted, "But the things that proceed out of the mouth come from the heart, and those defile the man" (Matthew 15:18).

- Then comes destruction. In the Old Testament, the term "the lamp" is used to describe a person's life, which in this verse is "wicked." The last line of Proverbs 21:4 could be summed up to state: The lifestyle of the arrogant is wicked, and their attitudes and actions are sinful.

We hear and read daily about heart disease. We eat for health in search of a low cholesterol reading. We determine to exercise in order to give our heart a workout and keep it strong and healthy. We even take prescription drugs that promise to counterbalance what we eat and our lack of exercise.

Yet we can so easily neglect the spiritual nature of our hearts. The starting—and ending—point for true humility is tending to your heart. And that begins with Jesus. He tells us to "Learn from Me, for I am gentle and humble in heart" (Matthew 11:29).

Pride undermines faith—" 'Proud,' 'Haughty,' 'Scoffer,' are his names, who acts with insolent pride" (Proverbs 21:24). Proverbs 18:12 tells us that pride leads to destruction. What kind of destruction? Proverbs 21:24 gives us the answer: A prideful person ultimately progresses to becoming a "scoffer," moving from being proud, to being haughty, to being a scoffer. The proud person soon becomes a mocker, who mocks at others, believing himself to be superior to all.[2] But the final step to scoffer is the most serious consequence of a prideful person because it reveals his attitude toward God. He scoffs and mocks at God!

The proud religious leaders of Jesus' day are a perfect example of the progression from proud to scoffer. They scoffed at Jesus throughout His ministry, and even as He hung dying on the cross. These same Jewish leaders scoffed at the coming of the Holy Spirit. They scoffed at the apostles as they spoke of Jesus as the Messiah. Later, the Greek philosophers scoffed as Paul spoke of Jesus and the resurrection when he addressed their assembly in Athens. And the proud are continuing to scoff today as they hear the gospel message.[3]

A proud person is insolent, boastful, and arrogant in their conceit. They have little or no use for God. The psalmist describes the proud person well: "The wicked, in the haughtiness of his countenance, does not seek Him. All his thoughts are, 'There is no God' " (Psalm 10:4).

By contrast, those who are humble are strengthened in their faith in God. The humble know that they need a Savior. They realize that salvation is by grace, not by merit. They know they didn't deserve God's salvation, so in humble adoration, they give God credit for everything they are and have, and for everything they do and will ever do.

Wow, what a wake-up call! Pride in any form is deadly. Maybe that's why pride and humility are so often spoken of in Proverbs.

If you are reading through Proverbs on a daily basis, you will most assuredly be getting either a daily warning against pride, or a daily exhortation to manifest humility. Proverbs is offering two paths and, therefore, two consequences.

I don't have to go very far in my thinking to come up with a perfect biblical example of a woman with the right attitude. Her name was Esther. She went from being an orphan to being the heroic queen of the Persian Empire. From start to finish in the book that bears her name, Esther was a humble servant of others. She repeatedly sought the advice of others. Throughout the book of Esther, we read that she "found favor" with those who knew her. In his book on the life of Esther, Charles Swindoll writes this about humility:

> We're never once commanded by God to "look" humble. Humility is an attitude. It is an attitude of the heart. An attitude of the mind. It is knowing your proper place...It is knowing your role and fulfilling it for God's glory and praise.[4]

Pride is to be hated—"The fear of the LORD is to hate evil; pride and arrogance and the evil way and the perverted mouth, I hate" (Proverbs 8:13). In this verse "Wisdom" is once again speaking. Her message is that those who desire to be godly—those who fear the Lord—hate evil. Pride is also hated by God: "Everyone who is proud in heart is an abomination to the LORD" (Proverbs 16:5). Pride is one of "six things which the LORD hates" (Proverbs 6:16-17). The message is clear: We should hate pride and any behavior in us that exposes it.

Are you wondering what you can do to pursue humility? A college student asked me the same thing. Believe me, it was a great exercise for me to think through her question and the

Bible's answers. It's been awhile, but here's the gist of what I shared with her:

- Pray, pray, pray! In prayer we bow our spirit before God as we think on Him. The same is true as we approach Him as our thrice-holy God. We are also humbled in ourselves as we confess and address our sin, as we praise and worship Him, as we give thanks to Him for His goodness to us, and as we humbly ask and request of Him what only He can give and accomplish. Even the posture of prayer is one of humility. Most people bow their head. Many kneel down to pray. And some lie prostrate.

- Refuse to talk about yourself. Instead, turn your thoughts away from yourself and send them upward toward God. Because you are dwelling on Him, you'll talk more about Him because He is what you are thinking about. Also, when you determine to talk less about yourself, that leaves you free and available to hear what someone else has to say and to learn more about them. You can engage in a conversation about the Lord and about the other person's problems and needs.

- Read, especially God's Word, but also books about the saints who have gone before you. Learn of their faith, their sufferings, their victories, how God strengthened them, comforted them, provided for them. Read of the trials and troubles experienced by martyrs for Christ. I have several books just on this topic of martyrs who have gone before us. What a humbling experience just reading about their lives and amazing grace!

Pride lures you into living independently—"Before destruction the heart of man is haughty, but humility goes before honor" (Proverbs 18:12). A prideful, arrogant person has such an inflated view of their own abilities that they don't want or need any input from anyone. They have no problem at all with using people, but they don't need people to help them.

This arrogant independence takes on an even more serious nature when this proud person thinks he or she can also live just fine without God. They depend on themselves rather than on God, and the result sooner or later will be "destruction."

The opposite is true of those who welcome God's presence and input into their life. Because they honor God and seek to live humbly, He honors them. When our hearts are filled with thoughts of God, there is no room left for dwelling on ourselves. When our hearts are obsessed with praising and worshipping God, there is no empty space left for us to talk about our little selves. With God in your life, there is no room for pride because His greatness and completeness make you aware of your own weak, sinful, needy self.

The Way Up Is Down

"A man's pride will bring him low, but a humble spirit will obtain honor" (Proverbs 29:23). Pride distorts our view of ourselves and others. A prideful person thinks they are "something" and therefore goes around demanding respect. Yet the man or woman who humbles himself and claims and demands "nothing," amazingly is honored and blessed.

God delights in reversing the way we naturally think as described by Jesus' statement: "Whoever exalts himself shall be humbled; and whoever humbles himself shall be exalted"

(Matthew 23:12) . Consider these people and their acts that signaled their humility. Also notice how they were exalted.

> Zacchaeus "came down" and found salvation (Luke 19:6).
>
> Mary Magdalene "stooped down" and saw the angels (John 20:11-12).
>
> The leper "kneeled down" and received cleansing (Luke 5:12).
>
> Peter "fell down" before Christ and was humbled (Luke 5:8).
>
> Mary "sat down" at the feet of Christ and learned the Lord's secrets (Luke 10:39).
>
> Christ "laid down" His life and thus He saved the sheep (John 10:15). [5]

Jesus Christ "came down" in order to save us...and take us up to heaven. Therefore, we bow down before Him today...and every day. Truly the way up is down. We must get down before we can go up. Until we are lost, we cannot be found. Until we are sinners, we cannot be saved. And even once we go up to heaven, we will bow down before the throne.[6]

God's Wisdom...for Your Day

The truths you just read about humility are so beautiful, so exquisite, so moving! But unfortunately, there is a struggle going on in our flesh. We know humility is the right choice, but we still so often choose to be prideful, boastful, and arrogant. What is the remedy for pride? Read on!

Every time we realize pride has raised its ugly head, we need to confess it and fall down on our knees—and stay down on our knees. The best way to avoid pride is to be constantly praying.

And while we are down on our knees, we can take the next step and ask God for His strength to avoid pride by seeking to live humbly and to nurture a heart of humility.

Pride is haughty, but humility is meek and lowly. Pride was manifested by Satan (see Isaiah 14:12-14), but humility was modeled by Jesus. Pride is exhausting because it is a totally self-manufactured emotion, but humility is a Spirit-manufactured emotion.

The Lord Jesus Christ is the supreme example of humility, and He asks us to follow in His steps, calling us to "take My yoke upon you and learn from Me, for I am gentle and humble in heart, and you will find rest for your souls" (Matthew 11:29).

30

Knowing God
—The Ultimate Goal—

Surely I am more stupid than any man,
and I do not have the understanding of a man.
Neither have I learned wisdom,
nor do I have the knowledge of the Holy One.
PROVERBS 30:2-3

A Prayer to Pray—

God of unsearchable greatness, there is one thing that deserves my most focused attention, that should call forth my greatest efforts. That is that I may know You and glorify You with all that is within me. Help me to understand that there is no true happiness, no fulfilling of Your purpose for me, apart from a life lived in and for Your Son and my Savior, the Lord Jesus Christ. Lead me to a greater knowledge of the Holy One. Amen.

As we step into Proverbs 30, we are wading into deep waters—a chapter that helps us know more deep truths about God, the Holy One, so we can better live our days and our lives His way. J.I. Packer, author of the classic book *Knowing God*, writes, "What higher, more exalted, and more compelling goal can there be than to know God?"[1]

As children of God, we heartily agree. Increased understanding of Almighty God is what you and I are seeking as we read through Proverbs each day, and through the entire Bible again and again. We pray and sing, "Lord, I want to know You," and the Bible is the only place where we find real information that increases our knowledge of God. That knowledge then improves our daily conduct and increases the depth of our worship.

Learning About God Requires Looking Upward

Throughout this book, I've been sharing my favorite verses from each chapter of Proverbs. I hope you've enjoyed the many two-line couplets in the book of Proverbs as you've been drawing wisdom from them. However, beginning in Proverbs 30 we will be reading whole passages with multiple verses which make up one key thought. And you will meet a new writer, Agur, who is hailed, praised, respected, and tagged as a sage who looked upward.[2]

When you read the first nine verses of Proverbs 30 as a unit, you will see right away that they are invaluable! They are gold—pure gold. That's because they give us such rich insight into knowing more about God. This is vitally important to you and me and all believers because our knowledge of God determines how we live out our days. What is required of us to know God more deeply and accurately?

Knowing God requires humility—"Surely I am more stupid than any man, and I do not have the understanding of a man. Neither have I learned wisdom, nor do I have the knowledge of the Holy One" (Proverbs 30:2-3). Here, by use of exaggeration, the human author of Proverbs 30 recognizes his own inability to claim that he has very much, if any, knowledge at all regarding God. He is openly and humbly admitting his ignorance.

Like the writer of Proverbs 30, the best way to start your day is to mentally—and even physically on your knees—acknowledge your own inability to understand the Person of God. Admit your lack—or slack—of dedication in pursuing your ultimate goal of seeking to gain a better understanding of God. Purpose to seek to know more about the God of heaven and earth. It will help you to live your day relying on God's abilities and resources. And best of all, it will help you to live your day looking upward.

Knowing God requires a submissive heart—Agur asked five questions. As you read them, focus on the answer to these questions and what the questions teach you about God!

> *Who has ascended into heaven and descended?*
> *Who has gathered the wind in His fists?*
> *Who has wrapped the waters in His garment?*
> *Who has established all the ends of the earth?*
> *What is His name or His son's name?*
> (Proverbs 30:4)

This is like reading poetry! Actually, it is biblical poetry, but these lofty thoughts and descriptions were written by Agur, "a man of faith who [was] an artist and an observer of character."[3]

The questions asked in verse 4 can have only one response

because they go beyond the reader's—and the writer's—ability to answer apart from responding with one word: "God!"

Spiritual growth in the knowledge of God requires three steps:

- Understand and admit your ignorance of God,
- Acknowledge your pride in thinking you know God, and
- Begin to contemplate the magnitude of God's power and might and mystery.

These humble and submissive acknowledgments take us back to Proverbs 1:7: "The fear of the LORD is the beginning of knowledge." Every day that you live looking upward in awe and reverence of God, in adoration and adulation of Him, and pursuing increased knowledge of the Holy One will be a day lived to the glory of God.

Knowing God requires believing His Word—"Every word of God is tested; He is a shield to those who take refuge in Him" (Proverbs 30:5). This verse helps us to know God by revealing two facts and truths about Him.

—Truth #1: We can trust God because we can trust His Word. Like a precious metal that has been certified or approved through the testing of fire, God's Word is true. It is totally inerrant and infallible, completely without error. As the psalmist wrote, "The words of the LORD are pure words; as silver tried in a furnace on the earth, refined seven times" (Psalm 12:6).

You can always, 100 percent of the time, trust that what you are reading in the Bible is a 100-percent accurate picture of God and His purposes and His will for you. Because the Bible is all of this and more, it is a sure guide for your daily life. Martin Luther testified, "The Bible is alive, it speaks to me; it has feet, it runs after me; it has hands, it lays hold on me."[4]

—Truth #2: We can trust God because "He is a shield to those who take refuge in Him." We can trust in His protection, which is perfect, thorough, and complete. As another proverb assures us, "In the fear of the LORD there is strong confidence" (14:26).

God's role in your safety, protection, and well-being is to be your shield and keep you safe. Your role is to trust Him, turn to Him, run to Him, and take refuge in Him when you are in danger and in need of protection. As nineteenth-century devotional writer Charles Bridges emoted, "Blessed trust, which brings a shield of special favor over His trembling child!...In all circumstances from within and from without—when I quake under the terrors of the law, in the hour of death, in the day of judgment—'Thou art...my shield.' "

Bridges later concluded, "Nothing honors God like this turning to Him in every time of need. If there is rest, peaceful confidence, safekeeping anywhere, it is here. Where is it found otherwise?"[5]

I can never think of God as my shield of protection without automatically thinking of one of my favorite psalms, which I quote to myself almost daily: "From the end of the earth I call to You when my heart is faint; lead me to the rock that is higher than I. For You have been a refuge for me, a tower of strength against the enemy" (Psalm 61:2-3).

Knowing God requires only His Word—"Do not add to His words or He will reprove you, and you will be proved a liar" (Proverbs 30:6). Don't you feel secure knowing that you don't need any other source outside of the Bible in order to know God? God's Word is sufficient. It is His personal record of who He is and all He has done—and will do—for you and His people.

John Wesley wrote, "All the knowledge you want is comprised in one book, the Bible," and Charles Wesley exhorted, "Be a person of one book—The Book." Both of these giants of the faith were referring to the Bible. Read it first. Read it foremost. And judge everything else you read and hear about God and living a godly life by what the Bible—the "one book"—says.

Knowing God gives you confidence to approach God—"Two things I asked of You, do not refuse me before I die..." (Proverbs 30:7-9). Are you shocked at the way Agur is addressing God, that he is actually demanding that God answer his requests? Keep in mind as we proceed to unravel these three verses that Agur spent his days observing and musing over God's sovereignty and His sufficiency (which Agur has expressed in verses 1-6).

By knowing *something* of God, Agur felt confident that he could approach God and ask two things of Him:

- He prayed to have good character: "Keep deception and lies far from me" (Proverbs 30:8). Notice Agur didn't pray for health, wealth, or power. Instead, he prayed in this way because he longed for godly integrity, godly character. He also knew that he needed strength to uphold that integrity whenever he was faced with deception, lies, and the myriad temptations that arise in daily living.

  Agur gives you and all believers solid advice for building solid character: You should long for integrity, pray for integrity, and pray specifically about avoiding the temptations that cause you to detour from God's holy will. You can begin by praying Jesus' words, "Our Father who is in heaven...do not lead us into temptation, but deliver us from evil" (Matthew 6:9,13).

- He prayed for circumstances that would not endanger his good character: "Give me neither poverty nor riches" (Proverbs 30:8). Agur knew that the two extremes of having "not enough" and having "more than enough" can lead to sin.

  For instance, you probably know from experience what it feels like to not have enough—which presents its own line of temptations. You could be tempted to steal or lie in order to have enough—which dishonors God. Also, when you don't think you have enough, you are tempted to malign God and wonder, "Where is God when I need Him? Can't He see we don't have enough? Why is He withholding His help? Doesn't He care?"

  The other temptation arrives when we have too much. If we have more than enough, we can easily slack off in our passion for God and our dependence upon Him to provide for us. We can be tempted to sin by forgetting about our need for God. And we can fall into the sin of pride by taking credit for our prosperity and our own ability to provide for ourselves without God's help.

Like Agur, when you know God more deeply, you long for godly integrity and for the strength to uphold that integrity—even when faced with the temptations of daily living.

Observing a Variety of Word Pictures

The first nine verses from Proverbs 30 are absolutely packed with God's "all-seeing comprehensive knowledge and power."[6] But, as you learned at the beginning of this chapter, Agur was "a man of faith who [was] an artist and an observer of character." In the remainder of chapter 30, he observes and "paints" colorful pictures of:

> the need for fairness for the underprivileged (10)
>
> the ugliness of arrogance (11-14)
>
> the nature of never-ending craving (15-17)
>
> the people or creatures or things that portray everything from those that are unbearable to those that are stately (16-31)
>
> the concluding call to humility (32-33)

God's Wisdom...for Your Day

Proverbs 30 gives us so much to ponder! So much to attempt to understand! So many reasons to worship the Holy One! So many truths about God that we can learn and treasure in our hearts!

How can you and I pursue the ultimate goal of knowing God? Do as Proverbs 30 instructs:

> Depend on God's Word completely.
> Dig deeply into God's Word daily.
> Depend on God's shield for protection.
> Draw near to God through prayer.
> Desire to live humbly before God.

Think now about Proverbs 30. This chapter began small with complaints of ignorance and a lack of the knowledge of God. Then it began to move steadily toward the ultimate goal of knowing God and reflecting on His majesty, greatness, and the knowledge of the Holy One.

As you read the closing to this chapter, notice Agur's progression *away from* his gripes and complaints and *toward* greater understanding of the truths of Almighty God. Then enjoy this devotional writer's summary of "the big picture."

> Agur was feeling overwhelmed, insignificant, and limited. But when he turned away from his own smallness to contemplate God's greatness, an atmosphere of confidence filled the rest of the chapter. He began with a little picture, no bigger than himself, but he soon looked at the big picture and forgot that he was weary and worn out. God gave him a new and refreshing point of view.[7]

Make this your habit, your pattern. Don't major on the minors. Force your eyes away from yourself and marvel at "the big picture"—God!

31

Becoming Beautiful in God's Eyes

—Excellence—

Charm is deceitful and beauty is vain,
but a woman who fears the L*ORD,*
she shall be praised.
PROVERBS 31:30

A Prayer to Pray—

O Changeless God, You are the same yesterday, today, and forever. As You were in the beginning, so You are now, and so You shall be throughout all eternity. Excellence describes You in all things. May I, too, live a life that strives for excellence in all things. Today may my choices, actions, and thoughts be those that characterize a woman who fears the Lord. Today may I bring honor and respect to Your holy name. Amen.

Privileged to join my husband on a three-week study trip through the Holy Land, I began to seriously wonder about halfway through our trek, "What was I thinking?" I was standing near the shore of the Dead Sea in Israel at the base of our next study topic—Masada, a massive natural fortress. I almost fell backward as I looked up, and up...and up! The steep path would take me 1300 feet—straight up—to the top!

Well, praise God, I made it to the top...only to have to make it back down later! That climb was so memorable that I wrote about it in my book *Beautiful in God's Eyes*.[1] I used that strenuous, upward climb as an example of God's lifetime goal and assignment for us as women to strive toward attaining the many virtues found and described in God's woman of excellence in Proverbs 31:10-31.

A Chapter with Two Portraits

Proverbs 31, the final chapter in Proverbs, God's book of wisdom, is for me both a comfort and a challenge. It has comforted me every day since the first time I read it because it set my feet on a sure path as a woman. I lived amidst utter confusion until I realized God—yes, God—was telling me in these 31 verses exactly how I should live. Still to this day, when I get up I know how God wants me to approach my day...and my life. I know my priorities—the priorities, example, and instruction He gives me in Proverbs 31.

And, oh, the challenge! I was ever-seeking something—anything!—that would bring me joy and fulfillment. That would give me purpose, that would be meaningful. Yet each fix or fad I was drawn to was fleeting. Maybe my latest venture was fun and gave me my next thrill. But when I discovered what God wanted of me and for me, I knew that by His grace I could make a difference every day as I followed God's plan and did what He asked of me.

An amazing picture is hand-delivered to you and me in Proverbs 31.

The portrait of the heart of a mother—Transport yourself back in time and eavesdrop on an intimate conversation between a wise mother and her young son. Verse 1 launches the 31 verses in Proverbs 31 by telling us a few things about the author and the messenger: "The words of King Lemuel, the oracle which his mother taught him." Here we see a portrait of a dedicated and devoted mom who imparted the wisdom that follows to her young son. She is teaching him the basics of right behavior in a man, and righteous leadership in a king (verses 2-9). She is passionately preparing her beloved boy—the young prince—to rule as a good and righteous king—a king with godly character.

Here's a brief outline of what this mother of the king-to-be poured into her son.

- Her son was precious to her. He was "the son of [her] womb" (repeated three times) and "the son of [her] vows," a son who had been dedicated to the Lord. Every child needs to know he or she is precious and fiercely loved by their mother.

- Her son, the future king, was not to engage in immorality, not to have multiple wives, and not to neglect or be distracted from his role of governing the people. Every child needs to be instructed, warned, and admonished about the consequences of veering away from God's perfect plan for marriage.

- Her son, the future king, was not to indulge in alcohol and drunkenness. Drinking was "not for kings...or for rulers." Every child needs to be educated regarding the disastrous results that accompany drinking. For a king or ruler, intoxication could cause him to forget what he had decreed and skew his reasoning and judgments.

- Her son, the future king, was to be a righteous judge, and to watch over and speak up for the concerns and rights of the poor and helpless. God makes His compassion for the poor clear in His law, and every child should be taught to own that same compassion.

This mother took God's law to heart. She did as God instructed in Deuteronomy 6:5-7:

> *You shall love the LORD your God with all your heart and with all your soul and with all your might. These words, which I am commanding you today, shall be on your heart. You shall teach them diligently to your sons and shall talk of them when you sit in your house and when you walk by the way and when you lie down and when you rise up.*

King Lemuel's mother taught her child God's standards and the godly virtues he would need for life. She taught him how to be a man of God and a leader of God's people. That's your calling, too, if you are a mother. Fill your heart with the things of God. Then out of that full heart teach your sons and daughters. Indeed, "The mother's heart is the child's schoolroom."[2]

In verses 10-31, this wise mother continues to teach and instruct her young son. In these verses, she describes the kind of wife her son, a soon-to-be king, should seek. He is to search for and marry a woman of excellent character, a woman whose heart is indeed a rare treasure: "An excellent wife, who can find? For her worth is far above jewels" (verse 10).

Perhaps because her son was so young, this clever mom arranged the qualities of an "excellent wife" using the Hebrew alphabet. This ABC-type arrangement could be quickly learned, easily memorized, regularly recited, was impossible to forget, and therefore permanently etched into the tablet of her boy's heart.

Enjoying the Heights of Proverbs 31:10-31

As I mentioned, I did reach the top of Masada. And, praise God, by His grace I did finish the book I was researching and writing on Proverbs 31—all 254 pages! I have to say, the wisdom and the word pictures and descriptions of the Proverbs 31 woman have guided me since my first reading through the book of Proverbs so many years ago. I shudder to think, "What if I had stopped reading Proverbs halfway through...and never made it to the end? What if I never read this final chapter of Proverbs about the many excellent character qualities God wants to see developed in me and in all His women?"

I was like the young boy whose mother was teaching the lessons recorded in Proverbs 31. Like that child, I knew next to nothing about the Bible. I grew up during the women's liberation movement and had adopted its defiant, rebellious views of a woman's roles in life. When I finished reading the 22 verses that describe what "a godly woman" is and does, a tremendous weight was lifted off my soul. I felt like I was standing at the heights of Masada with a clear and far-reaching view of how God wanted me to live every single day of my life. At last I had direction! I had the unchangeable Word of God. I had truth.

And in the Proverbs 31 woman of excellence, I had an example, a role model for life!

What Makes a Woman "Excellent"?

One of the dozens of noteworthy contributions made by the Proverbs 31 woman was the leadership she exhibited in her home. Although she was married to a leader in the community, we get the strong impression that she managed the home and made many important decisions concerning her family's welfare. There's no doubt her husband was a man of power, but this woman was "the power behind the man"! He took care of matters governing the city, while she took care of matters governing the home.

What makes this woman so special? In a word, "character." This entire book featuring "Proverbs for a Woman's Day" has been about character. About virtues. About the virtues God desires, extols, and expects in His women. Just look at the Contents page and see the list! And it's only a partial list. Here in Proverbs 31, the positive character qualities we've witnessed throughout the book of Proverbs seem to be rolled up into this one excellent woman—the Proverbs 31 woman. Not only is she an excellent mother, she is also:

An Excellent Woman

- She works diligently—She "works with her hands in delight" and "stretches out her hands to the distaff, and her hands grasp the spindle" (verses 13,19).

- She takes care of her home—"She looks well to the ways of her household, and does not eat the bread of idleness" (verse 27).

- She acts properly—"Strength and dignity are her clothing" (verse 25).

An Excellent Wife

- She seeks her husband's good—"She does him good and not evil all the days of her life" (verse 12).

- She keeps his confidence—"The heart of her husband trusts in her" (verse 11).

- She complements his position—"Her husband is known in the gates, when he sits among the elders of the land" (verse 23).

An Excellent Homemaker

- She clothes her family royally—"All her household are clothed with scarlet" (verse 21).

- She watches over her family—She "gives food to her household" and "she looks well to the ways of her household" (verses 15,27).

- She shops wisely—"She brings her food from afar" (verse 14).

An Excellent Businesswoman

- She is creative—"She makes linen garments and sells them" (verse 24).

- She networks with others—She "supplies belts for the tradesmen" (verse 24).
- She is confident in her work—"She senses that her gain is good" (verse 18).
- She has a plan and a dream—"She considers a field and buys it; from her earnings she plants a vineyard" (verse 16).

An Excellent Neighbor

- She gives to the poor—"She extends her hand to the poor" (verse 20).
- She helps the needy—"She stretches out her hands to the needy" (verse 20).
- She speaks wisely and with kindness—"She opens her mouth in wisdom, and the teaching of kindness is on her tongue" (verse 26).

God's Wisdom...for Your Day

The marvelous woman described in these 22 verses is often despised and scorned in our present-day culture. Satan and the fallen world have painted this noble woman, who is so very beautiful in God's eyes, as something old-fashioned, ridiculous, and laughable. Today prayerfully read through Proverbs 31 again. Ask God, the Lord of all wisdom, to show you this woman's worth. Look afresh at the true, stunning beauty of this for-real lady. Stand in awe as you take in the beautiful portrait of this exquisite woman. God has put her here for all time so you will always have a model of what He wants you to live and model that is beautiful in His eyes.

As we close this chapter with verse 31, we see her reward: "Give her the product of her hands, and let her works praise her in the gates."

Like you, this woman had a role among the people and blessed her community. She sold her homemade items to bring in income, and planted and tended a vineyard she purchased with the funds she had earned and saved. She was quite the businesswoman.

One key message that is loud and clear in Proverbs 31:10-31 is that character is key. Excellence is the result of character, and character is nurtured every day, in every choice made.

Another key message this remarkable woman sends to us across the centuries is this: Inside your home—whether it be a mansion, an apartment, a mud hut on the mission field, or a recreational vehicle—no task is too meaningless or any effort too small to merit your focus. The world may scoff and laugh at the Proverbs 31 woman, but it doesn't matter because her true praise comes from God. And isn't that the praise you are yearning for? Instead of worrying about what the world thinks is important, focus on your very own little place called home. Then you—as God's excellent woman—shall be praised for...

...your merit—"Her worth is far above jewels" (verse 10).

...your devotion—"Her children rise up and bless

her; her husband also, and he praises her" (verse 28).

...your reputation—"You excel them all" (verse 29).

...your strength—"Strength and dignity are her clothing" (verse 25).

...your devotion to God—"A woman who fears the LORD, she shall be praised" (verse 30).

When Matthew Henry closed his devotional commentary on Proverbs 31, he wrote beautifully in the language of his day: "Thus is shut up this looking-glass for ladies, which they are desired to open and dress themselves by; and if they do so, their adorning will be found to praise, and honour, and glory, at the appearing of Jesus Christ."[3]

Appendix 1

Getting the Most Out of Proverbs

As a teen in high school, I loved English literature and I loved reading poetry. I was such a romantic! In my classes I learned that English poetry is based on rhyme and meter. But when I started reading Proverbs, I realized that Proverbs was a different kind of poetry than I had been exposed to in school. English poetry contains sonnets or many long groups of verses, but Proverbs is mainly made up of short, concise statements that give us God's wisdom and rules for life quickly in a few memorable words.

The Structure of Proverbs

Here is some technical information that will help you understand the proverbs you read and make sure you get the most out of each proverb. Because Proverbs is ancient Hebrew poetry, it does not depend upon rhyme for its appeal. Rather, it depends upon parallelism. There are six types of parallelism found in the book of Proverbs. Once I learned to recognize these different structures, my understanding took a great leap forward! The "riddles" in Proverbs became more clear.

- Synonymous proverbs: The first line states a fact, and the fact is repeated in the second line, both lines essentially saying the same thing. The second line usually starts with the word "and," as in Proverbs 1:5 and 11:25:

A wise man will hear and increase in learning,
and a man of understanding will acquire wise counsel.

The generous man will be prosperous,
and he who waters will himself be watered.

- Antithetical proverbs: The first line states a positive fact, and the second line states the opposite or negative fact. The second line usually starts with the word "but," as in Proverbs 3:33 and 10:7:

  The curse of the LORD is on the house of the wicked,
  but He blesses the dwelling of the righteous.

  The memory of the righteous is blessed,
  but the name of the wicked will rot.

- Synthetic proverbs: The first line addresses a subject, and the second line gives further information on that same subject. The second line can include or begin with "and," as in Proverbs 10:18 and 9:13:

  He who conceals hatred has lying lips,
  and he who spreads slander is a fool.

  The woman of folly is boisterous,
  she is naive, and knows nothing.

- Integrated proverbs: The first line begins a subject, and the second line completes the subject. For instance, in Proverbs 22:6 you read:

> *Train up a child in the way he should go,*
> *even when he is old he will not depart from it.*

- Parabolic proverbs: The first line begins with a vivid word picture from life, and the second line gives a related analogy, as seen in Proverbs 11:22 and 25:3:

  > *As a ring of gold in a swine's snout*
  > *so is a beautiful woman who lacks discretion.*

  > *As the heavens for height and the earth for depth,*
  > *so the heart of kings is unsearchable.*

- Comparative proverbs: The first line contains a statement that is then compared with a second statement. Many comparative proverbs are often referred to as the "better than" proverbs, as seen in Proverbs 12:9 and 15:16:

  > *Better is he who is lightly esteemed and has a servant*
  > *than he who honors himself and lacks bread.*

  > *Better is a little with the fear of the LORD,*
  > *than great treasure and turmoil with it.*

Two Additional Structures of Proverbs

Readers are usually delighted by these two additional types of proverbs. They also give the readers an easy way to remember the instructions in the proverbs.

- Numerical proverbs: This is a group or section of proverbs that begins with numbers which identify them as numerical proverbs: "There are six things which the LORD hates" as seen in Proverbs 6:16-19. In the case of Proverbs

30:15-31, the number of comparisons switches from two—"The leech has two daughters," to three—"There are three things that will not be satisfied," to four—"Four things are small on the earth."

- Acrostic proverbs: Proverbs 31:10-31 is an acrostic group or section of proverbs referred to as "The Excellent Woman." Each of the 22 verses starts with a successive letter of the Hebrew alphabet.

Appendix 2

Authors and an Outline of Proverbs

Because Proverbs 1:1 states, "The proverbs of Solomon the son of David, king of Israel," readers usually assume the book of Proverbs was written by one author—Solomon. Actually, there are several authors. Besides Solomon, who wrote the majority of the proverbs, there were also:

The sayings and "words of the wise" (22:17-24),
"The words of Agur" (chapter 30), and
"The words of King Lemuel" (chapter 31).

Who was Solomon? He was the wisest, most wealthy, and most highly esteemed king of his time. God used Solomon to complete the building of the temple and as a righteous judge of the people. As the son of David (who was a man after God's own heart—Acts 13:22), Solomon had much to share because God blessed Solomon with wisdom when he asked for wisdom instead of riches and honor (2 Chronicles 1:10). The Bible says Solomon spoke 3000 proverbs (1 Kings 4:32), but not all of these are recorded in the book of Proverbs.

In a technical sense, God Himself is the divine author of all the proverbs in the book of Proverbs—and of the entire Bible.

God breathed all of the many wonderful and instructive proverbs and words of wisdom that make up this priceless, inspired-by-God book of wisdom (2 Timothy 3:16) by using Solomon and others.

A Structural Outline of Proverbs

Part One—The Virtues of Wisdom (Proverbs 1–9)

These chapters give an extensive treatment of the subject of "Wisdom," using the image of a father extolling the virtues of wisdom and challenging his son to live a life of wisdom. These proverbs are in the form of a teaching discourse.

Part Two—The Proverbs of Solomon (Proverbs 10:1–22:16)

This section contains 375 contrasting proverbs (10:1–15:33) and synonymous proverbs (16:1–22:16) which are attributed to Solomon. This section is what most people are familiar with when they think of Proverbs—two parallel lines of verse either contrasting each other or agreeing with each other.

Part Three—The Sayings of the Wise (Proverbs 22:17–24:34)

This section contains the proverbs of "the wise," or 30 wise sayings. The style of this section returns to the pattern of chapters 1–9, which was proverbial discourse.

Part Four—Proverbs Copied by Hezekiah's Men (Proverbs 25:1–29:27)

These are more proverbs of Solomon, collected by good King Hezekiah 300 years after Solomon's death. Like Solomon's first set of proverbs, these are the two-line parallel type proverbs.

Part Five—The Words of Agur (Proverbs 30)

Since Agur or his father, Jakeh, are unknown, some translators suggest that these are not actual people but could be translated "gatherer" or "collector" of proverbs.[1] This chapter is more like the book of Ecclesiastes than of any other sections of Proverbs. The words are dark sayings, born of sorrow and defeat, forming questions rather than answers.[2]

Part Six—The Words of Lemuel (Proverbs 31:1-9)

As with Agur, we have no knowledge of King Lemuel. But we do have the concerns and instruction of a godly mother that she passed down to her son. She warned her beloved son about two vices: illicit sex and excessive alcohol.

Part Seven—The Picture of the Excellent Woman (Proverbs 31:10-31)

This section could have been written by Lemuel or could be an anonymous appendix or epilogue to the book of Proverbs. It is an alphabetic acrostic, meaning each of its 22 verses begins with a consecutive letter of the Hebrew alphabet. The 22 verses are like pearls strung together to produce an attractive necklace of grace and beauty. (For a more in-depth treatment of these verses, see *Beautiful in God's Eyes*[3] and *Discovering the Treasures of a Godly Woman.*[4])

Bibliography

Alden, Robert L. *Proverbs: A Commentary on an Ancient Book of Timeless Advice.* Grand Rapids, MI: Baker Book House, 1990.

Eims, Leroy. *Wisdom from Above—for Living Here Below.* Wheaton, IL: Victor Books, 1981.

George, Elizabeth. *Beautiful in God's Eyes: The Treasures of the Proverbs 31 Woman.* Eugene, OR: Harvest House Publishers, 1998.

George, Elizabeth. *Discovering the Treasures of a Godly Woman—Proverbs 31.* Eugene, OR: Harvest House Publishers, 2003.

Goldbert, Louis, Th.D. *Wisdom for Living—Bible Book Studies—Proverbs.* Chicago, IL: Moody Correspondence School, 1983.

Kidner, Derek. *Proverbs: An Introduction and Commentary.* Downers Grove, IL: InterVarsity Press, 1973.

MacDonald, William. *Enjoying the Proverbs.* Kansas City, KS: Walterick Publishers, 1982.

Mayhue, Richard. *Practicing Proverbs: Wise Living for Foolish Times.* Ross-shire, Scotland: Christian Focus Publications, 2003.

McLellan, Vern. *Proverbs for People.* Eugene, OR: Harvest House Publishers, 1983.

Santa, George F. *A Modern Study in the Book of Proverbs: Charles Bridges' Classic Revised for Today's Reader.* Milford, MI: Mott Media, 1978.

Spence, H.D. and Exell, Joseph S. *The Pulpit Commentary, Volume 9—Proverbs, Ecclesiastes, Song of Solomon.* Grand Rapids, MI: Wm. B. Eerdmans Publishing Company, 1978.

Swindoll, Charles R. *Wisdom for the Way: Wise Words for Busy People.* Nashville, TN: J. Countryman, a division of Thomas Nelson, Inc., 2001.

Turner, Charles W. *Studies in Proverbs: Wise Words in a Wicked World.* Grand Rapids, MI: Baker Book House, 1981.

Voorwinde, Steven. *Wisdom for Today's Issues: A Topical Arrangement of the Proverbs.* Phillipsburg, NJ: Presbyterian and Reformed Publishing Company, 1981.

Wardlaw, Ralph. *Lectures on the Book of Proverbs, Volumes 1–3.* Minneapolis, MN: Klock & Klock Christian Publishers, Inc., 1981.

Wiersbe, Warren W. *Be Skillful: Tapping God's Guidebook to Fulfillment.* Colorado Springs, CO: Chariot Victor Publishing, division of Cook Communications, 1995.

Wilson, Neil S. *The One Year Book of Proverbs.* Wheaton, IL: Tyndale House Publishers, Inc., 2002.

Notes

1: Beginning Your Every Day—Wisdom

1. George F. Santa, *A Modern Study in the Book of Proverbs* (Milford, MI: Mott Media, 1978), p. 2.
2. See Genesis 1:1,26-27; Ezra 7:25; Job 21:22.
3. See Psalm 119:98-100.
4. See Proverbs 2:2-6.

2: Parenting with Passion—Childraising

1. William MacDonald, *Enjoying the Proverbs* (Kansas City, KS: Walterick Publishers, 1982), p. 50.
2. Cheryl Julia Dunn, *A Study of Proverbs 31:10-31*, master thesis (Biola University, 1993), p. 144.
3. John MacArthur, *The MacArthur Study Bible* (Nashville, TN: Nelson Bibles, 2006), p. 867.

3: Finding Peace in a World of Chaos—Trusting God

1. See Hebrews 12:6-8.
2. See Proverbs 1:7; 2:5; 3:7.

4: Guarding Your Heart—Watchfulness

1. J.D. Douglas, *The New Bible Dictionary*, organizing editor (Grand Rapids, MI: Wm. B. Eerdmans Publishing Co., 1978), p. 509.

5: Being a Faithful Wife—Marriage

1. Drawn from Neil S. Wilson, *The One Year Book of Proverbs* (Wheaton, IL: Tyndale House Publishers, Inc., 2002), June 5.

8: Leading a Life Marked by Wisdom—Success

1. Many believe that Jesus Himself is referred to in Proverbs 8:22-29. However,

while Jesus is the revelation of God's wisdom (1 Corinthians 1:24) and possesses all wisdom and knowledge (Colossians 2:3) and assisted in creation, there is no indication that these verses are a direct reference to Christ.

9: Creating a Place Called Home—Homemaking

1. See *A Woman After God's Own Heart* by Elizabeth George (Eugene, OR: Harvest House Publishers, 2006) for the history of the "pink marker" and "pink passages."
2. See Proverbs 24:3-4.
3. Curtis Vaughan, ed., *The Word: The Bible from 26 Translations*—Moffit (Gulfport, MS: Mathis Publishers, Inc., 1991), p. 1178.
4. Robert L. Alden, *Proverbs: A Commentary on an Ancient Book of Timeless Advice* (Grand Rapids, MI: Baker Book House, 1990), p. 80.

10: Blessing Others with Your Speech—Mouth

1. William MacDonald, *Enjoying the Proverbs* (Kansas City, KS: Walterick Publishers, 1982), p. 58.
2. Elizabeth George, *Beautiful in God's Eyes* (Eugene, OR: Harvest House Publishers, 1998).

11: Enriching Your Character—Virtues

1. See Proverbs 10:12 and 1 Peter 4:8.
2. See *A Woman After God's Own Heart* by Elizabeth George (Eugene, OR: Harvest House Publishers, 2006).

12: Growing Smarter Each Day—Teachable

1. See Titus 2:3-5. You may also want to read Elizabeth's book *A Woman's High Calling* (Eugene, OR: Harvest House Publishers, 2001).
2. John MacArthur, *The MacArthur Study Bible*—NASB updated edition (Nashville, TN: Nelson Bibles, 2006), p. 876.
3. William MacDonald, *Enjoying the Proverbs* (Kansas City, KS: Walterick Publishers, 1982), pp. 51-52.
4. See Matthew 13:45-46.
5. Neil S. Wilson, *The One Year Book of Proverbs* (Wheaton, IL: Tyndale House Publishers, Inc., 2002), May 12.

13: Speaking the Truth—Words

1. Benjamin Franklin, *Poor Richard's Almanac*, vol. 1, "Lists to Live By," p. 322.
2. Bruce B. Barton, David R. Veerman, and Neil Wilson, *Life Application Bible*

Commentary—James (Wheaton, IL: Tyndale House Publishers, Inc., 1992), pp. 80-81.

3. Ibid.
4. See Proverbs 6:16-19.
5. Curtis Vaughan, *The Word—The Bible from 26 Translations*, citing *The New Testament in Basic English* (Gulfport, MS: Mathis Publishers, Inc., 1991), p. 1182.
6. *Handbook of Life Application*, p. 655, James 3:5.
7. M.R. DeHaan and Henry G. Bosch, *Our Daily Bread* (Grand Rapids, MI: Zondervan Publishing House, 1982), January 20.
8. *Checklist for Life for Women*, "Watch Your Mouth" (Nashville, TN: Thomas Nelson Publishers, 2002), p. 305.

14: Walking in Obedience—Confidence

1. See Proverbs 1:7,29; 2:5; 8:13; 9:10; 10:27; 14:2,26-27; 15:16,33; 16:6; 19:23; 22:4; and 23:17.
2. Albert M. Wells, Jr., *Inspiring Quotations—Contemporary & Classical*, citing Richard Halverson (Nashville, TN: Thomas Nelson Publishers, 1988), p. 73.
3. Derek Kidner, *Proverbs* (Downers Grove, IL: InterVarsity Press, 1964), p. 117.
4. Neil S. Wilson, *The One Year Book of Proverbs* (Wheaton, IL: Tyndale House Publishers, Inc., 2002), December 15.
5. John MacArthur, *The MacArthur Study Bible*, NASB updated edition (Nashville, TN: Nelson Bibles, 2006), p. 877.
6. *The Holy Bible*, New Living Translation (Wheaton, IL: Tyndale House Publishers, Inc., 1996).

15: Enjoying the Benefits of Wisdom—Choices

1. Curtis Vaughan, *The Word—The Bible from 26 Translations*, citing Knox translation (Gulfport, MS: Mathis Publishers, Inc., 1991), p. 1198.
2. Derek Kidner, *The Proverbs* (Downers Grove, IL: InterVarsity Press, 1973), p. 115.

17: Being a Good Friend—Friendship

1. *Checklist for Life for Teens* (Nashville, TN: Thomas Nelson Publishers, 2002), p. 35.

18: Finding Something Good—A Wife After God's Own Heart

1. Derek Kidner, *The Proverbs: An Introduction and Commentary* (Downers Grove, IL: InterVarsity Press, 1973), p. 133.

2. Robert L. Alden, *Proverbs* (Grand Rapids, MI: Baker Book House, 1990), p. 145.

19: Conquering Your Worst Enemy—Anger

1. See Colossians 3:8.
2. M.R. DeHaan, M.D. and Henry G. Bosch, editor and coauthor, *Bread for Each Day—365 Devotional Meditations* (Grand Rapids, MI: Zondervan, 1980), May 28.

20: Getting All the Advice You Can—Counsel

1. See Proverbs 11:14; 12:15; 15:22; 20:18.
2. See 1 Corinthians 11:3; Ephesians 5:22-23; Colossians 3:18; 1 Peter 3:1.

21: Planning—and Living—Your Day God's Way—Life Management

1. *Life Application Bible—The Living Bible* (Wheaton, IL: Tyndale House Publishers, Inc., 1988), p. 946.

22: Training Up a Child for God—Parenting

1. Benjamin R. DeJong, *Uncle Ben's Quotebook* (Grand Rapids, MI: Zondervan Publishing House, 1977), p. 142, no author's name given.

23: Choosing What You Eat and Drink—Health

1. *The Shorter Westminster Catechism.*
2. Derek Kidner, *The Tyndale Old Testament Commentaries—Proverbs* (Downers Grove, IL: InterVarsity Press, 1964), p. 152.
3. Curtis Vaughan, general editor, *The Word: The Bible in 26 Translations* (Gulfport, MS: Mathis Publishers, Inc., 1991), p. 1246.
4. Simon J. Kistemaker, *New Testament Commentary—1 Corinthians* (Grand Rapids, MI; Baker Books, 1993), p. 358.

24: Following God's Plan for Success—Diligence

1. See Isaiah 40:29-31 and 1 Kings 19:5-8.

25: Being Faithful in All Things—Dependability

1. See Luke 23:49–24:10.
2. See 2 Corinthians 5:20.
3. See 2 Corinthians 3:2-3.
4. Elizabeth George, *A Woman's Walk with God* (Eugene, OR: Harvest House Publishers, 2000).

26: Getting Rid of Laziness—Personal Discipline

1. See Proverbs 31:15,17,18,27.

27: Being Careful in a Careless World—Common Sense

1. Robert L. Alden, *Proverbs: A Commentary on an Ancient Book of Timeless Advice* (Grand Rapids, MI: Baker Book House, 1990), p. 192.
2. Neil S. Wilson, *The One Year Book of Proverbs* (Wheaton, IL: Tyndale House Publishers, Inc., 2002), June 12.

28: Cultivating a Generous Heart—Finances

1. Roy B. Zuck, *The Speaker's Quote Book,* citing *Bits & Pieces* (Grand Rapids, MI: Kregel Publications, 1997), p. 259.
2. See Proverbs 10:2; 13:11; 20:21; 21:6; 28:22.
3. Frank S. Mead, ed., *12,000 Religious Quotations* (Grand Rapids, MI: Baker Book House, 2000), p. 309.
4. *Checklist for Life—The Ultimate Handbook* (Nashville, TN: Thomas Nelson Publishers, 2002), p. 52.

29: Humbling Yourself Before God—Humility

1. William MacDonald, *Enjoying the Proverbs* (Kansas City, KS: Walterick Publishers, 1982), p. 155.
2. See Proverbs 1:22; 9:8; 13:1; 15:12; 19:25.
3. See John 6:42; Matthew 27:39-40; Acts 2:13; 4:17-18; 13:44; 17:1-34; 1 Corinthians 2:14.
4. Charles R. Swindoll, *Esther: A Woman of Strength and Dignity* (Nashville: W Publishing Group, quoted in *Great Attitudes for Graduates!* [Nashville: J. Countryman, Thomas Nelson, 2006], p. 160.)
5. M.R. DeHaan and Henry G. Bosch, ed. and coauthor, *Our Daily Bread—366 Devotional Meditations* (Grand Rapids, MI: Zondervan Publishing House, 1959), February 29.
6. Ibid.

30: Knowing God—The Ultimate Goal

1. Online quote.
2. Derek Kidner, *The Proverbs: An Introduction and Commentary* (Downers Grove, IL: InterVarsity Press, 1978), p. 178.
3. Derek Kidner, *The Proverbs: An Introduction and Commentary* (Downers Grove, IL: InterVarsity Press, 1978), p. 178.

4. Albert M. Wells, Jr., editor, *Inspiring Quotations—Contemporary & Classical* (Nashville, TN: Thomas Nelson Publishers, 1988), p. 15.
5. Charles Bridges, *A Modern Study in the Book of Proverbs,* revised by George Santa (Milford, MI: Mott Media, 1978), pp. 703-04.
6. Robert Jamieson, A.R. Fausset, and David Brown, eds., *Commentary on the Whole Bible* (Grand Rapids, MI: Zondervan Publishing House, 1971), p. 473.
7. Neil S. Wilson, *The One Year Book of Proverbs* (Wheaton, IL: Tyndale House Publishers, Inc., 2002), January 30.

31: Becoming Beautiful in God's Eyes—Excellence

1. Elizabeth George, *Beautiful in God's Eyes* (Eugene, OR: Harvest House Publishers, 1998).
2. M.R. DeHaan and Henry C. Bosch, ed. and coauthor, *Our Daily Bread,* citing Henry Ward Beecher (Grand Rapids, MI: Zondervan, 1959), May 8.
3. Matthew Henry, *Commentary on the Whole Bible* (Peabody, MA: Hendrickson Publishers, Inc., 1991), p. 1027.

Appendix 2: Authors and an Outline of Proverbs

1. Robert L. Alden, *Proverbs: A Commentary on an Ancient Book of Timeless Advice* (Grand Rapids, MI: Baker Book House, 1990), p. 207.
2. Ibid.
3. Elizabeth George, *Beautiful in God's Eyes* (Eugene, OR: Harvest House Publishers, 1998).
4. Elizabeth George, *Discovering the Treasures of a Godly Woman* (Eugene, OR: Harvest House Publishers, 2003).

Books by Elizabeth George

- 15 Verses to Pray for Your Husband
- Beautiful in God's Eyes
- Breaking the Worry Habit…Forever
- Finding God's Path Through Your Trials
- Following God with All Your Heart
- The Heart of a Woman Who Prays
- Life Management for Busy Women
- Loving God with All Your Mind
- Loving God with All Your Mind DVD and Workbook
- A Mom After God's Own Heart
- A Mom After God's Own Heart Devotional
- Moments of Grace for a Woman's Heart
- One Minute with the Women of the Bible
- One-Minute Inspirations for Women
- Proverbs for a Woman's Day
- Quiet Confidence for a Woman's Heart
- Raising a Daughter After God's Own Heart
- The Remarkable Women of the Bible
- Small Changes for a Better Life
- Walking with the Women of the Bible
- A Wife After God's Own Heart
- A Woman After God's Own Heart®
- A Woman After God's Own Heart®—
- Daily Devotional
- A Woman's Daily Walk with God
- A Woman's Guide to Making Right Choices
- A Woman's High Calling
- A Woman's Walk with God
- A Woman Who Reflects the Heart of Jesus

Bible Studies

- Becoming a Woman of Beauty & Strength
- Cultivating a Life of Character
- Discovering the Treasures of a Godly Woman
- Embracing God's Grace
- Experiencing God's Peace
- Growing in Wisdom & Faith
- Living with Passion and Purpose
- Nurturing a Heart of Humility
- Pursuing Godliness
- Putting On a Gentle & Quiet Spirit
- Relying on the Power of the Spirit
- Understanding Your Blessings in Christ
- Walking in God's Promises

Study Guides

- Beautiful in God's Eyes Growth & Study Guide
- Following God with All Your Heart Growth & Study Guide
- Life Management for Busy Women Growth & Study Guide
- Loving God with All Your Mind Growth & Study Guide
- Loving God with All Your Mind Interactive Workbook
- A Mom After God's Own Heart Growth & Study Guide
- The Remarkable Women of the Bible Growth & Study Guide
- Small Changes for a Better Life Growth & Study Guide
- A Wife After God's Own Heart Growth & Study Guide
- A Woman After God's Own Heart® Growth & Study Guide
- A Woman Who Reflects the Heart of Jesus Growth & Study Guide
- A Woman's High Calling Growth and Study Guide

Books for Young Women

- Beautiful in God's Eyes for Young Women
- A Young Woman After God's Own Heart
- A Young Woman After God's Own Heart—A Devotional
- A Young Woman's Guide to Discovering Her Bible
- A Young Woman's Guide to Making Right Choices
- A Young Woman's Guide to Prayer
- A Young Woman Who Reflects the Heart of Jesus
- A Young Woman's Walk with God

Books for Tweens

- A Girl After God's Own Heart
- A Girl After God's Own Heart Devotional
- A Girl's Guide to Discovering Her Bible
- A Girl's Guide to Making Really Good Choices
- You Always Have a Friend in Jesus for Girls

Children's Books

- God's Wisdom for Little Boys
- God's Wisdom for Little Girls
- A Little Boy After God's Own Heart
- A Little Girl After God's Own Heart

Books by Jim George

- 10 Minutes to Knowing the Men and Women of the Bible
- 50 Most Important Teachings of the Bible
- The Bare Bones Bible® Handbook
- The Bare Bones Bible® Handbook for Teens
- Basic Bible Pocket Guide, The
- A Boy After God's Own Heart Action Devotional
- A Boy After God's Own Heart
- A Boy's Guide to Discovering His Bible
- A Boy's Guide to Making Really Good Choices
- A Dad After God's Own Heart
- A Husband After God's Own Heart
- Know Your Bible from A to Z
- A Leader After God's Own Heart
- A Man After God's Own Heart
- A Man After God's Own Heart Devotional
- The Man Who Makes a Difference
- One-Minute Insights for Men
- The Remarkable Prayers of the Bible
- You Always Have a Friend in Jesus for Boys
- A Young Man After God's Own Heart
- A Young Man's Guide to Discovering His Bible
- A Young Man's Guide to Making Right Choices

Books by Jim & Elizabeth George

- A Couple After God's Own Heart
- A Couple After God's Own Heart Interactive Workbook
- God's Wisdom for Little Boys
- A Little Boy After God's Own Heart

To learn more about Harvest House books and to read sample chapters, visit our website:

www.harvesthousepublishers.com

HARVEST HOUSE PUBLISHERS
EUGENE, OREGON

Elizabeth George

A Woman After God's Own Heart®

Over 1,000,000 Sold

"Our transformation into being a woman after God's own heart

is indeed God's work. But what I offer are the disciplines we can follow to place ourselves before God—disciplines regarding our devotional life, our husband, our children, our personal growth, and our ministry—so that He can do that work in our heart. I invite you to join me as each of us seeks to become the woman God calls and empowers us to be."

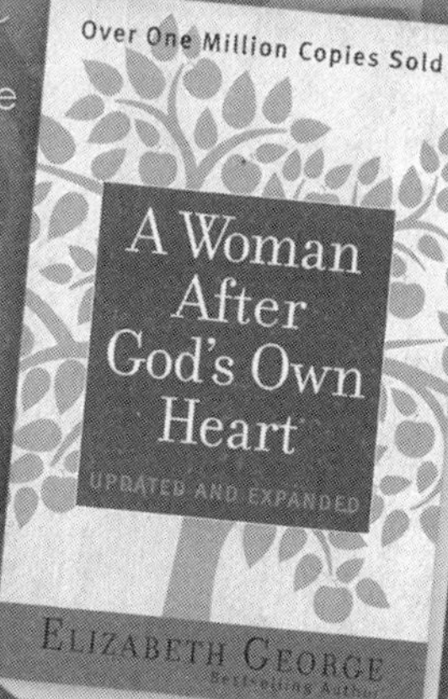

Book ISBN 978-0-7369-5962-9
Growth & Study ISBN 978-0-7369-5964-3

A Woman After God's Own Heart
A DEVOTIONAL
ELIZABETH GEORGE

Elizabeth draws on wisdom from her bestselling books, popular radio spots, and podcasts to provide uplifting, dynamic, relevant devotions for today's women. You'll find plenty of encouragement and practical ideas to help you get the most out of life.

Beautifully designed, pocket-sized, with a padded cover make this a great gift.

ISBN 978-0-7369-5966-7

HARVEST HOUSE PUBLISHERS
EUGENE, OREGON

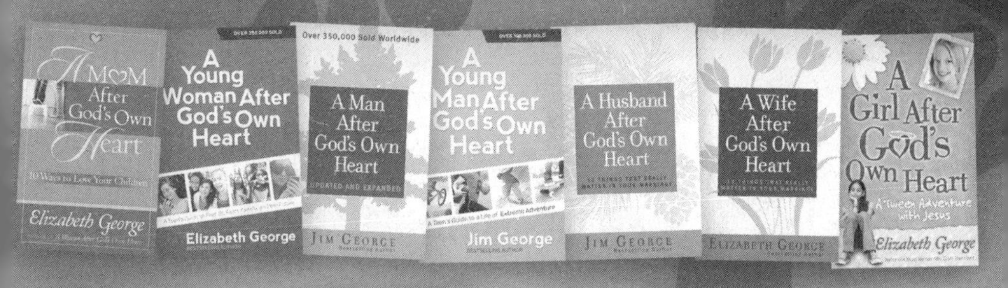

AVAILABLE AT BOOKSTORES EVERYWHERE
Read a sample chapter at www.harvesthousepublishers.com

About the Author

Elizabeth George is a CBA and ECPA bestselling author of more than 100 books and Bible studies (more than 11 million sold). As a writer and speaker, her passion is to teach the Bible in a way that changes women's lives. For information about Elizabeth's books and to sign up for her newsletter and blogs, please contact Elizabeth at:

www.ElizabethGeorge.com

YouTube

goodreads